1993

THE RISE OF ANCIENT ISRAEL

On the cover: **Bronze bull figurine.** *Looming large despite its diminutive (4-inch-high by 7-inch-long) size, this bronze bull may come from the only Israelite cultic site yet discovered dating to the 12th century B.C.E. Found at the summit of a high ridge near biblical Dothan, in the Samaria hills north of Mt. Ebal, the bull may have been an offering or it may have been worshiped as a deity. El, the chief Cannanite god, was often depicted as a bull. If the ridge near Dothan is indeed Israelite, it is noteworthy that the only Israelite shrine from the 12th century B.C.E. contains a figurine almost identical to earlier depictions of the Canaanite deity El.*

THE RISE OF ANCIENT ISRAEL

Symposium at the Smithsonian Institution
October 26, 1991

Sponsored by the Resident Associate Program

HERSHEL SHANKS

WILLIAM G. DEVER

BARUCH HALPERN

P. KYLE MCCARTER, JR.

BIBLICAL ARCHAEOLOGY SOCIETY
Washington, DC

Contents

14/61/ 30

List of Illustrations

List of Color Plates

The Lecturers

Hershel Shanks is founder and editor of *Biblical Archaeology Review* and *Bible Review*. He is the author of *The City of David* (Bazak, 1973), a guide to biblical Jerusalem, and *Judaism in Stone* (Harper & Row, 1979), tracing the development of ancient synagogues. He edited *Recent Archaeology in the Land of Israel* (Israel Exploration Society, 1984) with Professor Benjamin Mazar; *Ancient Israel: A Short History From Abraham to the Roman Destruction of the Temple* (Prentice-Hall, 1988), the two-volume *Archaeology and The Bible: The Best of Biblical Archaeology Review* (BAS, 1990), *The Dead Sea Scrolls: After Forty Years* (BAS, 1991) and *Understanding the Dead Sea Scrolls* (Random House, 1992). A graduate of Harvard Law School, he has also published widely on legal topics.

Baruch Halpern is professor of ancient history and religious studies and chair of Jewish Studies at Pennsylvania State University. He is the author of *The First Historians—The Hebrew Bible and History* (Harper & Row, 1988), *The Emergence of Israel in Canaan* (Scholars Press, 1983), *The Constitution of the Monarchy in Israel* (Scholars Press, 1981) and is currently writing a history of ancient Israel for the Anchor Bible Reference Library.

William G. Dever is professor of Near Eastern archaeology at the University of Arizona. From 1971 to 1975 he was director of the William Foxwell Albright Institute of Archaeological Research in Jerusalem. He directed the excavations at Gezer for six consecutive seasons from 1966 to 1971 and in 1984. He is editor of the *Annual of the American Schools of Oriental Research* and among his many publications are *Recent Archaeological Discoveries and Biblical Research* (University of Washington Press, 1990) and *Recent Excavations in Israel: Studies in Iron Age Archaeology* (American Schools of Oriental Research, 1989), co-edited with Seymour Gitin.

P. Kyle McCarter, Jr., is the William Foxwell Albright Professor of Biblical and Ancient Near Eastern Studies at the Johns Hopkins University in Baltimore, Maryland. Prior to going to Johns Hopkins in 1985, he taught for 11 years at the University of Virginia. His books and other publications include commentaries on 1 Samuel and 2 Samuel in the Anchor Bible series published by Doubleday. He is currently preparing a new edition and translation of the Copper Scroll from Qumran (3Q15) to be published by Princeton University Press.

HERSHEL SHANKS

Defining the Problems

Where We Are in the Debate

e're going to hear today from three world-class scholars on what may be the hottest topic in biblical studies—the rise of ancient Israel—or, as the scholars like to call it, the *emergence* of ancient Israel—a little fancier term.

Where did the people who became the nation of Israel come from? And when? By what process did they become a nation? What were their religious roots? How did they find their God Yahweh?

Scores of scholars are struggling with these issues. Some of the disagreements are intense. Our speakers today are among the leaders in the debate. We may hear from them whether any kind of consensus is emerging.

My job is simply to provide the *mise-en-scène*, to set the stage, so that the scholars who follow me will be able to leap into their subject with an assuredly knowledgeable audience. For many of you, what I say will be elementary; for some of you, it won't, and I want to bring everybody up to speed.

By the time I finish, you will be able to distinguish very easily between the Late Bronze Age and Iron Age I (laughter), you will know what the Merneptah Stele is, you will be able to talk about a four-room house and a collared-rim jar and the three models of the Israelite emergence in Canaan.

I'm also going to try to provide a little context for you, so that you'll have in mind the larger picture, the basic framework within which the more focused discussion of the next three speakers will take place.

In doing that, I will weave back and forth between the biblical text and the archaeological materials. Because, as some of you know, I shun controversy (laughter), I will present to you only what is unequivocally true and acceptable to everyone. So, what I say, therefore, you can accept. When the next speakers get up, you will hear the more controversial and iffy research. (Laughter.)

Let's begin with the Bible.

The Bible begins with the creation of the world and proceeds in the first ten chapters of Genesis to give us a world history—until everyone but Noah and his family are destroyed in a flood. God's first experiment in creating a world of worthy people fails.

So he destroys it and starts all over again. These early chapters of Genesis culminating in the Flood have nothing to do with Israel. In fact, this story provides a contrast with the second attempt to create worthy people. This time God chooses a single family.[1] He concentrates on this family—the family of Abraham, the first Hebrew. The rest of the Book of Genesis is the story of this family—first Abraham and his wife Sarah, their son Isaac and his wife Rebecca, their son Jacob and his wives Rachel and Leah and, finally, Jacob's 12 sons, who become the 12 tribes of Israel. They go down to Egypt and settle in the Delta when a famine grips Canaan. Fortunately for the family, one of the sons, who had preceded the others under difficult circumstances, has risen to a position of authority second only to the pharaoh himself.

It is in Egypt that Israel becomes a people—or at least numerous enough to be a people. There they multiply and in the end are enslaved by a pharaoh who "knew not Joseph." Finally, they escape under the leadership of a man named Moses. They then begin their 40-year trek to the Promised Land. On the way, they experience a theophany at a place called Sinai—or sometimes Horeb. There God gives them a set of laws by which to live. The people enter into a covenant with God in which they agree to obey his laws and in return they become his people, the recipient of his benefices. After their 40-year sojourn in the desert, they arrive, finally, at the Promised Land.

Now at this point the Bible gives us two somewhat different accounts of how they took possession of the Promised Land. The first is in the last part of the Book of Numbers and the Book of Joshua. The second and somewhat different account is in the Book of Judges.[2]

The account in Joshua portrays a lightning military campaign—lasting less than five years. In this campaign, the various peoples of Canaan are defeated; "Joshua defeated the whole land, the hill country and the Negev and the lowland and the slopes and all their kings" (Joshua 10:40). After these victories, the land west of the Jordan is allotted among the Israelite tribes.

The account in Judges is quite different. First of all, the order is reversed. In Judges, the allotment comes first, and after the allotment they attempt to take possession of the land by conquest. In Judges there is no unified effort by "all Israel" to conquer the land, as seems to be the case in Joshua. In Judges the effort to possess the land seems to be the work of individual tribes or groups of related tribes.

And most important, Judges makes it clear that by no means was the entire land subdued. In Judges 1 as a matter of fact is a list of 20 cities whose people were not driven out by the newcomers. These cities included Jerusalem, Gezer, Megiddo, Taanach, Beth-Shean and Beth Shemesh (Judges 1:21,27-33). These are some of the most important cities in the country. So we have quite a difference here between the Book of Joshua and the Book of Judges.

Now the events in Judges do purport to occur after the death of Joshua, so the two accounts can be harmonized somewhat by assuming that the picture in Joshua is exaggerated and that the military victories recorded there were not quite so extensive or complete as they are described.

In any event, it's clear that the account in Judges does preserve a tradition that the land of Canaan was possessed over a long period of time. And, if we look carefully, there are hints of this even in the Book of Joshua.

During this period, the Israelites are threatened by various Canaanite peoples, but charismatic military leaders called Judges always arise and save them. Eventually, however, this loose Israelite tribal confederacy proves inadequate to defend itself against the Philistine threat. Some more organized structure is needed, so the people ask for a king. And they get a king. Saul is appointed, but his reign is ultimately a failure. He is replaced by Israel's most glorious king, David, and with his reign, Israel truly becomes a nation.

This, in brief, is the biblical account.

Until the 20th century, the emergence of Israel in Canaan was almost always referred to as the "conquest of Canaan," for the Bible clearly portrays it this way. And indeed until after the Second World War, it was generally thought that archaeology supported this view. For a time, archaeology was the darling of the nursery among those who regarded the Bible as literally true.

JULIUS WELLHAUSEN. A strange genius, this 19th-century (1844-1918) German scholar inaugurated modern biblical scholarship by asserting that the Pentateuch, or five books of Moses, is comprised principally of four strands. These four he designated J (for Yahwist; Jahwist in German), E (for Elohist), P (for the priestly code) and D (for the Deuteronomist). These components, in Wellhausen's view, were joined together and edited by R, the redactor.

In a reaction to Wellhausen's theories, archaeology became—for a time—the darling of biblical literalists. In the first half of the 20th century, just as the view that the Bible was written by humans during discernible historical periods was gaining ground among scholars, the newly emerging field of archaeology appeared to be validating a key tenet of the Bible: At site after site archaeologists were uncovering destruction levels that seemed to prove that the Israelites conquered Canaan in a swift military campaign as described in the Book of Joshua.

To explain this, I've got to give a little of the history of biblical scholarship. In the 19th century, we have a burgeoning of historical, critical biblical scholarship. The impetus is often associated with a strange genius by the name of Julius Wellhausen. He shattered the calm of biblical literalists by breaking down the Pentateuch into four different authorial strands. These different strands of authorship are often designated by the familiar letters J, E, P and D. J stands for the Yahwist (Jahwist in German), E for the Elohist, P for the priestly code and D for the Deuteronomist. These were all put together by a fellow designated R, for the redactor—a fancy name for editor.

All this was very disturbing to biblical literalists. And at this point—in the first half of the 20th century—archaeology seemed to come to the rescue. The short of it is that in tell after tell, archaeologists found a destruction level that they thought they could identify with the Israelite conquest of Canaan.

Well, archaeology is no longer a crutch in this classic sense of the conquest model. We simply can no longer posit a series of destructions in Canaan that can rationally be identified as the result of the Israelite conquest. Recently, our archaeological methodology has improved, we can date levels much more securely and more sites have now been excavated. As a result, we can no longer say that archaeology supports what we may call the conquest model of Israel's emergence in Canaan.

Some sites like Jericho and Ai appear to have been uninhabited at the time Joshua was supposed to have conquered them. Other sites, like Gibeon, that the Bible says the Israelites conquered, do not have appropriate destruction levels. But most important is that if you start jiggling around dates of the various sites where there are destruction levels, you can't fit them together. The time and space paths of destruction levels don't fit. The fact is that destructions occur not only because Israelites were there, but for various other reasons as well. As a result of all this, the conquest model has fallen into disfavor.

Many modern scholars, wanting to be in the forefront of things, have simply written off the idea of an Israelite conquest. But my advice is don't be so quick to write it off completely. I'll come back to this later.

When the failings of the conquest model were exposed, it was

ALBRECHT ALT (1883-1956), a German biblical scholar, proposed that the ancient Israelites, rather than conquering Canaan militarily, peacefully infiltrated the hill country of Canaan; the Israelites later came into conflict with the Canaanites in the more fertile, and hence more desirable, valleys and plains.

Recent archaeological surveys—the practice of examining the surface of wide areas, in contrast to the intensive excavation of a single site—reveal that the central hill country of Canaan was sparsely populated during the Late Bronze Age (1550-1200 B.C.E.); by Iron Age I (1200-1000 B.C.E.), the time most commonly accepted by scholars for the emergence of Israel, however, more than 200 new sites had sprung up. Proponents of the infiltration model conclude that a new people—the Israelites—entered the hill country about 1200 B.C.E.

replaced in the minds of many scholars by the second model, the so-called peaceful infiltration model. This model is often associated with the name of the great German biblical scholar Albrecht Alt. According to this theory, the central hill country of Canaan, where the Bible says the Israelites settled, was almost empty at the time the Israelites entered Canaan. So the Israelites could readily infiltrate quite peaceably—and this, in the view of those who support this theory, was precisely what they did. The scholars who rely on this theory naturally looked for support in the Book of Judges, although part of this theory was that as the Israelites extended farther into the land of Canaan, they bumped up against the Canaanites. That is, the better locations of the fertile valleys and in the plains were already occupied by the Canaanites. Then there were some military clashes. But basically that was later and the initial settlement was a peaceful one.

Archaeology has provided considerable support for this view—most importantly in the settlement pattern in the central hill country.

L et's look at the archaeology a bit. Archaeologists have divided time into various periods, supposedly based on cultural discontinuities. They see a difference, a sharp break, in the cultural, material record. It's really not the case, but we have to divide time into periods. The two big periods for our purposes are the Bronze Age and the Iron Age. They got their names because it was supposed that bronze was the predominant metal in the Bronze Age and iron in the Iron Age. That's not really true, but it's too late to rename the periods. (Laughter.) For some reason, the Bronze Age was divided into Early, Middle and Late and the Iron Age was divided into Iron I and II; why the difference I don't know.

What we're going to be talking about is the Late Bronze Age and Iron I. That's the transition from Bronze to Iron. When I use those terms I'm talking about dates, not metals. Archaeologists are pretty much agreed on the absolute dates of the Late Bronze Age and Iron Age I. The Late Bronze Age extended from about 1550 to about 1200 B.C.E. Iron I extended from about 1200 to—there's some difference here, but I like to use the date of 1000 B.C.E. because that's approximately when David's reign begins and the Israelite monarchy is firmly established. So the transition between Late Bronze and Iron I is 1200 B.C.E. And that's about the beginning of Israel's emergence in Canaan. And it goes through Iron I to the monarchy—that's the end of Iron I.

One of the more recent developments in archaeological methodology is the archaeological survey. You all know what a tell is—the remains of a buried city on different levels, called strata. In an archaeological survey, instead of excavating the tell of a buried city, the archaeologists survey a wide area, looking on the surface for every bit of evidence they can find of ancient occupation, occasionally excavating a small site, but usually it does not include the excavation of major tells. The results of these archaeological surveys have often been quite remarkable.

What these surveys have shown is that the central hill country of Canaan was very sparsely settled in the Late Bronze Age, which would have provided the open area for Alt's peaceful Israelite infiltration. And in fact in Iron I over 200 new sites sprang up in this previously relatively empty central hill country. Obviously, there was a new population here. I'm going to illustrate this in the territory of Manasseh, which was surveyed by an Israeli archaeologist, Adam Zertal.* The Late Bronze settlements are few and primarily in the valleys and the better locations. The Iron I settlements are very numerous. There is the presence of an entirely new population in

---

* See Adam Zertal, "Israel Enters Canaan—Following the Pottery Trail," *Biblical Archaeology Review*, September/October 1991.

the central hill country.

Moreover, the new settlers brought with them a new style of architecture and a peculiarly decorated storage jar. The new architecture is called the four-room house. But that, again, is a misnomer. Anybody who can find four rooms in this plan of this four-room house will be making a mistake (laughter) because they will misidentify the four rooms. It's not really a four-room house, but let's not confuse things now. (Laughter.) A four-room house consists of a long narrow room; sticking out from that are three long rooms. So that the four rooms are the long narrow room at the

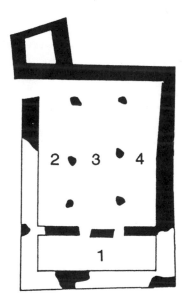

A FOUR-ROOM HOUSE from 'Izbet Sartah. Shown here is the plan of a house type new to early Iron Age central Canaan and thought until recently by archaeologists to have been a key clue to dating the emergence of the Israelites.

In its simplest form, a four-room house consisted of a long, narrow room (1, at bottom of plan), with three rooms (2, 3, 4), separated by pillars, jutting from it. In practice, however, the rooms in houses such as this were often subdivided, with additional rooms built along the periphery. The middle of the three rooms (3) was probably not roofed over but was left open to serve as a courtyard; this area probably contained an oven. The inhabitants most likely lived in and slept on a second-floor level, with the first floor holding animals. Some archaeologists prefer to call these structures pillared houses.

FOUR-ROOM HOUSE AT 'IZBET SARTAH. One of the earliest Israelite settlements, 'Izbet Sartah sits on the western edge of the Canaanite hill country. The site presents an obvious problem: If the Israelites entered Canaan from the east—whether by conquest or through peaceful infiltration—how could one of their earliest settlements be so far to the west, which should have been the last area to be settled?

Weak points in the conquest and the peaceful infiltration models highlighted by sites such as 'Izbet Sartah and the ambiguous evidence presented by four-room houses and collared-rim jars led some scholars to advance a third proposal: the peasant revolt model. Supported most notably by the scholars George Mendenhall and Norman Gottwald, this model argues that the people we now think of as the Israelites were originally for the most part Canaanite peasants who had taken to the hill country after having revolted against their urban overlords at the end of the Late Bronze Age. Once established in the hill country, these former peasants developed a religion based on the worship of Yahweh and evolved into the people called Israel.

bottom and the three long ones sticking from it. The reason it's an obvious misnomer is that the four rooms are often subdivided, and other rooms may be added on the periphery. But the basic structure is a four-room plan. Another reason why it's a misnomer is that the middle room of the three is a courtyard that isn't roofed—it had no roof on it. It probably had an oven in it. And there was probably a second floor where the family actually lived and slept. On the first floor they kept the animals. But this at least gives an idea of what is meant by a four-room house. [Harvard professor] Larry Stager, who is excavating Ashkelon, prefers to call these houses pillared houses. That's probably more accurate, but the four-room moniker has stuck. And that's the common name for them.

At one time, the four-room house was considered a peculiarly Israelite style of architecture, but we will soon see that this is not necessarily true.

The settlers in the hill country also had a new kind of storage jar that is called a collared-rim jar. The collar is right around the shoulder, just below the neck of the vessel. It's a little decorative element. It doesn't have a function. And at one time this was thought to be a style of Israelite pottery. If you found the collared-rim jars in an excavation this was an indication that it was an Israelite context, but this too is not necessarily true.

But you can see the picture that is emerging—new inhabitants occupying the sparsely settled hill country—just the area that the

COLLARED-RIM JARS. The presence of large storage jars such as these at Canaanite hill-country sites had until recently been considered a second indication—the other being four-room-house architecture—of Israelite habitation. Distinguished by a collar-like ridge at the top of its short, wide neck, these jars could typically hold 10 to 15 gallons of water. Some archaeologists have suggested that collared-rim jars were the principal means of moving and storing water in the area until about 1000 B.C.E. The widespread use of iron tools at that time made possible the digging of cisterns in bedrock; collared-rim jars fell into disuse, victims of technological progress.

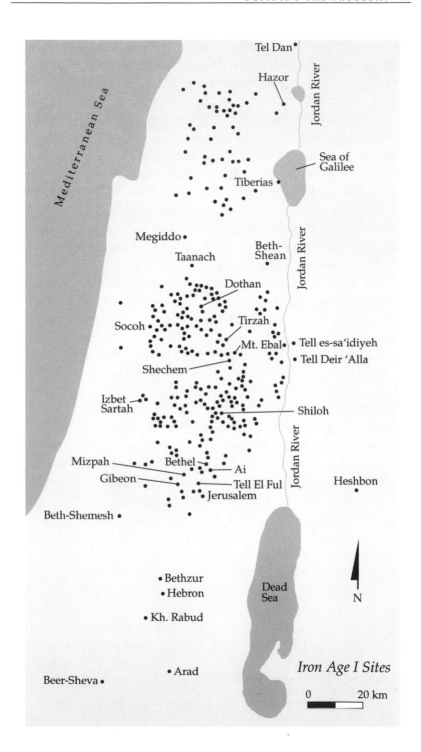

Mediterranean Sea

Tel Dan

Hazor

Jordan River

Sea of
Galilee

Tiberias

Jordan River

Megiddo

Beth-
Shean

Taanach

Dothan

Tirzah

Socoh

Mt. Ebal

Tell es-sa'idiyeh

Tell Deir 'Alla

Shechem

Izbet
Sartah

Shiloh

Jordan River

Mizpah

Bethel

Ai

Gibeon

Tell El Ful

Jerusalem

Heshbon

Beth-Shemesh

Bethzur

Hebron

Dead
Sea

N

Kh. Rabud

Arad

Iron Age I Sites

Beer-Sheva

0   20 km

Bible says the Israelites settled in when they crossed the Jordan—and a special kind of architecture and a special style of pottery. It is very tempting to say that here we have the incoming Israelites.

But is this enough to call these people Israelites? Many scholars don't think it is. For example, some of these four-room houses have been found outside the areas supposedly settled by the Israelites, including sites east of the Jordan. Moreover, antecedents of this architecture can be found among the earlier Canaanites.

As for the collared-rim jars, the use of these particular vessels may simply reflect needs of anyone living in the hill country to transport water. The collared-rim jar does not necessarily reflect ethnicity. It may simply reflect the peculiar needs of anyone—Israelite or Canaanite—living in the hill country.

I confess that I don't find either of these arguments very convincing, but that's beside the point.*

In any event, doubts about the peaceful infiltration model of Israelite settlement led to the development of a third model, generally known as the peasant revolt model—again not a very happy moniker, for reasons we will soon see. This third—and last—model was pioneered by a University of Michigan scholar named George Mendenhall in the mid-1960s. According to this model, the Israelites emerged not from outside Canaan, but from inside. In short, the Exodus from Egypt, if there was one, was minuscule. According to this theory, the people who became known as Israelites were really peasants who revolted against their urban overlords in the Late Bronze Age cities of Canaan. These peasants then fled to the hills, where under the ideological guidance of a deity called Yahweh they developed and expanded into a people called Israel.

This theory has been considerably developed and expanded by a New York Theological Seminary professor named Norman Gottwald.** Professor Gottwald agrees with Mendenhall that the Israelites developed from within Canaanite society, but, consistent with his Marxist orientation, Gottwald contends that the reason for the split from the Late Bronze Age urban centers was economic, not

* See Hershel Shanks, "Yigal Shiloh—Last Thoughts," *Biblical Archaeology Review*, May/June 1988.
** See "Israel's Emergence in Canaan—BR Interviews Norman Gottwald," *Bible Review*, October 1989.

theological.* In short, the emergence of Israel can be found in a social revolution at the end of the Late Bronze Age.

The peasant revolt model has proved to be a very pregnant one for many scholars. For one thing, it is based on anthropological and sociological analogies from other societies in which new cultures have emerged.

It also appeals to some scholars who find the biblical account of Israel's emergence in Canaan historically worthless. According to these scholars, there is simply no history to be gleaned from the biblical accounts which purport to relate what happened regarding Israel before the monarchy. At best, these scholars say, this is simply a national history created to give Israel a pedigreed past. Some scholars go further and contend that there is no reliable history in the Bible until the Exile to Babylon.

Scholars who accept the peasant revolt model also rely on archaeological evidence. For example, they point to Canaanite antecedents of the four-room house and the collared-rim jar. And it is undoubtedly true that there are cultural continuities between Late Bronze and Iron I Canaan, although there are often differences too.

The proponents of the peasant revolt model also point to a settlement like the one at a site called 'Izbet Sartah.** It is in the far west, at the edge of the hill country, overlooking the coastal plain. It is one of the earliest of the new Iron I settlements. Yet if the Israelites came from outside and from the east (the other side of the Jordan), 'Izbet Sartah should be one of the last places to be settled.

Whatever the validity of the peasant revolt model, it has starkly raised the issue—much debated among scholars—as to whether the emergence of Israel was an inside or an outside job, whether Israel came from outside Canaan or from inside Canaan. It used to be that scholars almost always accounted for major cultural changes by the introduction of a new ethnic element coming in from the outside. No longer is this the fad. So the scholars of Israelite history are asking themselves, did Israel emerge from within Canaanite society or did Israel come into the land from outside? We are likely to hear more about this from Bill Dever later in this program.

* See Bernhard Anderson, "Mendenhall Disavows Paternity," *Bible Review*, Summer 1986.
** See Moshe Kochavi and Aaron Demsky, "An Israelite Village from the Days of the Judges," *Biblical Archaeology Review*, September/October 1978.

These then are the three models of Israel's emergence in
Canaan—the conquest model, the peaceful infiltration model
and the peasant revolt model (or perhaps, more accurately,
the social revolution model). But in the last few years scholars have
moved beyond these models. It is no longer a matter of plumping
for one or the other model. We have entered a period of synthesis
and variation. The models have become kind of "ideal types" in the
Weberian sense. In reality, they don't exist in these pure forms.

No clear consensus among scholars has evolved. A lot of new
ideas are swirling around. There is much debate. What the outcome
will be, I, for one, cannot even predict.

On the one hand, there are those scholars who say that the
Bible is absolutely worthless as a source for the history of
premonarchical Israel. They look to sociology and anthropology and,
to some extent, archaeology, to develop an accurate historical sce-
nario. They often begin with the undoubted archaeological fact that
almost the entire then-known world was in turmoil and upheaval at
the end of the Late Bronze Age. Egyptian authority was slipping; the
Sea Peoples, including the Philistines, were fleeing from the Aegean
area, attacking Egypt and other areas, finally settling in Cyprus and
coastal Canaan; the Hittite empire in Asia Minor and north Syria
was fragmenting and turning to a bunch of small warring city-states;
this was the time of the Trojan War, a time when the great coastal
city of Syria, Ugarit, was destroyed, never to be rebuilt.

What caused all this turmoil? Climatic changes? Drought? War?
Economic dislocations? The Dorian invasion of Greece? No one
seems to know, for sure. But according to the peasant revolt, or
social revolution, theory, the coastal cities of Canaan also suffered
and declined, their feudal social structures collapsed and the urban
underclass took to the hills where they eventually emerged as Israel.

At the other end of the scholarly spectrum are those who contend that there were surely military aspects to Israel's emergence in
Canaan and that this must be part of any synthesis. Among those
who take this position is eminent biblical scholar Frank Cross of
Harvard.

Abraham Malamat of Hebrew University has emphasized the
extraordinarily realistic and clever military strategies that the Bible
says the Israelites employed in their successful defeat of major walled

Canaanite cities.* In not a single case was there a frontal attack in daylight. Instead, because they were essentially outclassed militarily, the Israelites employed stratagems. They used decoys and ambushes, night attacks and surprise attacks, spies and infiltrators. They took advantage of the topography in a remarkably realistic way. This suggests to many that there must be a core of historical reality to these accounts even though the details and numbers are exaggerated and the whole thing is recounted as seen through a theological lens.

As we have seen, the Bible often preserves more than one tradition of an event, as in the Book of Joshua and the Book of Judges with respect to Israel's subjugation of the Promised Land. But, as Yigael Yadin has pointed out, only a single tradition of Israel's origin has been preserved—that they came from outside Canaan, from Egypt, where they were slaves. Who would invent such an ignominious past?**

Bryant Wood has recently reexamined the archaeological evidence relating to the destruction of Jericho.† There was a destruction at Jericho. All archaeologists agree on this. But when did it occur? The most recent and most famous excavator of Jericho, the British archaeologist Kathleen Kenyon, dated this destruction to the Middle Bronze Age—after which the site was abandoned. Thus, she said, there was no city here for Joshua to conquer at the end of the Late Bronze Age. This view has been widely accepted and has posed a major problem for the conquest model. In his careful reexamination of the archaeological data, not only from Kenyon's excavations but also from earlier excavations, Wood has shown that this destruction at Jericho occurred in uncanny detail just as the Bible describes it. There was a strong wall there, just as the Bible says. And the wall even came tumbling down, according to the archaeological evidence. Actually there were two walls around the city—the main city wall at the top of the tell and a revetment wall lower down. Outside this revetment wall, Kenyon found piles of red mudbricks that had fallen from the city wall at the top of the tell and then tumbled down the

---

* See Abraham Malamat, "How Inferior Israelite Forces Conquered Fortified Canaanite Cities," *Biblical Archaeology Review*, March/April 1982.

** See Yigael Yadin, "Is the Biblical Account of the Israelite Conquest of Canaan Historically Reliable?" *Biblical Archaeology Review*, March/April 1982.

† See Bryant Wood, "Did the Israelites Conquer Jericho? A New Look at the Archaeological Evidence," *Biblical Archaeology Review*, March/April 1990.

slope, piling up at the base of the revetment wall. (Or the bricks could have been on top of the revetment wall and tumbled down from there; the difference is insignificant. The fact is they came together in a heap outside the revetment wall). The amount of bricks piled up there was enough for a wall 6.5 feet wide and 12 feet high.

These collapsed bricks then formed a kind of ramp that an invading army could have used to go up into the city. And sure enough, the Bible tells us that the Israelites who encircled the city "went up into the city, every man straight before him" (Joshua 6:20).

Moreover, the wall could have tumbled as a result of an earthquake. Earthquake activity is well known in this area: Jericho sits right in the Great Rift on the edge of a tectonic plate.

Kenyon found that the city was destroyed in a fiery conflagration: the walls and floors were blackened or reddened by fire. But, she adds, "the collapse of the walls of the eastern rooms seems to have taken place before they were affected by the fire." This was the sequence of events in the biblical account of Jericho's conquest: The walls fell down and *then* the Israelites put the city to the torch.

The archaeologists also found heaps of burnt grain in the houses—more grain than has ever been found in any excavation in what was ancient Israel. This indicates two things: First, the victory of the invaders must have been a swift one, rather than the customary siege that would attempt to starve out the inhabitants (the biblical victory was of course swift). Second, the presence of so much grain indicates that the city must have been destroyed in the spring, shortly after the harvest. That is when the Bible says the attack occurred. There is another strange thing about the presence of so much grain. A successful invading army could be expected to plunder the grain before setting the city on fire. But the army that conquered Jericho inexplicably did not do this. The Bible tells us that the Lord commanded that everything from Jericho was to be destroyed; they were to take no plunder.

One last item, the Bible tells us that the attacking Israelites were able to ford the Jordan easily because the river stopped flowing for them; the water above Jericho stood up in a heap (Joshua 3:16). This has actually happened on several occasions in modern times. At this point the Jordan is not a mighty stream. It has been stopped up by mud slides and by material that fell into it in connection with earthquakes. The water actually ceased flowing for between 16 hours and two days, as recorded in 1927, 1906, 1834 and on three even earlier occasions.

So what do we make of all this?

One way to deal with it is to say that the Israelites somehow had a memory of this early destruction of Jericho and incorporated it into their own theologically oriented history, even though it was not actually the Israelites that did the conquering.

Another way is to attribute the destruction of Jericho to the Israelites. This requires either that you move the Israelite conquest back to the Middle Bronze Age or that you reinterpret the archaeological evidence so that you attribute the destruction to the Late Bronze Age instead of to the Middle Bronze Age. Both of these things have been attempted, although most scholars reject these efforts to attribute Jericho's destruction to the Israelites.

This brings me to the question of dating, about which I will say only a few words. Most archaeologists are agreed that if there is archaeological evidence for the emergence of Israel in Canaan, it must be at the beginning of the Iron Age, about 1200 B.C.E.

Yet there is also evidence that there was an important people called Israel living in Canaan as early as the late 13th century B.C.E. I'm referring to the famous Merneptah Stele found in Thebes at the end of the last century. The Merneptah Stele is a black granite slab over 7.5 feet high, covered with hieroglyphic writing. Mainly it recounts the exploits of Pharaoh Merneptah during his Libyan campaign, but at the end he also recalls his earlier victories in a military campaign in Canaan.

Now there are two universally agreed facts about this stele. One is that it dates to 1207 B.C.E. Second, it mentions Israel in connection with this earlier campaign in Canaan. There in hieroglyphic writing is the earliest extra-biblical mention of Israel. This is what it says:

> "Canaan has been plundered into every sort of woe;
> Ashkelon has been overcome;
> Gezer has been captured.
> Yanoam was made nonexistent;
> Israel is laid waste, his seed is not."

"CANAAN HAS BEEN PLUNDERED INTO EVERY SORT OF WOE;" declares the
Merneptah Stele, *"Ashkelon has been overcome; Gezer has been captured. Yanoam
was made nonexistent; Israel is laid waste, his seed is not."* Near the bottom of the
stele, Merneptah also trumpets his earlier campaigns in Canaan at the beginning
of his reign.

       The mention of Israel—the earliest non-biblical reference—occurs slightly
to the left of center in the second line from the bottom (detail below). Unpronounced
signs, called determinatives, attached to the place names in this section of the stele
indicate that Ashkelon, Gezer and Yanoam were cities and that Canaan was a foreign
land; the determinative for Israel, however, indicates that the term referred to a people
rather than a place. The Merneptah Stele shows that a people called Israel existed in
1212 B.C.E. and that the pharaoh of Egypt not only knew about them but also felt it
was worth boasting about having defeated them in battle.

Now there are a couple of things I want to say about this mention of Israel.

This is not just a mention in a deed or a contract that may have reference to a small village or even less. This reference to Israel shows that the most powerful man in the world, the pharaoh of Egypt, was aware of Israel. Not only was he aware of Israel—he boasts that one of the most important achievements of his reign was to defeat Israel. Of course he exaggerates when he says that Israel's seed is not. We know that even today, 3,200 years later, that seed is still growing and thriving. But that is beside the point. The fact is that in 1212 B.C.E. (the campaign was five years before the inscription), Israel must already have been a military force to be reckoned with. And this is right in that transition period between the Late Bronze Age and Iron I.

The next point I want to make about the Merneptah Stele, which is sometimes also called the Israel Stele, requires us to talk a little about hieroglyphics. In hieroglyphic writing there are some signs that are not pronounced; they indicate the kind of word to which they are attached. The unpronounced signs are called determinatives. So, in the quotation I read to you from the Merneptah Stele, where the pharaoh was victorious over four entities in Canaan, each entity, in addition to the signs indicating how the word is pronounced, also has attached to it a determinative that tells us what kind of word it is. Attached to three of the four entities—Ashkelon, Gezer and Yanoam—is a determinative that tells us that they are cities. The determinative attached to Canaan, which introduces the set of four, is the determinative for a foreign land. The determinative attached to Israel, however, is for a people. In other words, in 1207 B.C.E. Israel was a people in Canaan important enough not only to be known to pharaoh, but important enough for him to boast that he defeated them militarily.

The Merneptah Stele is obviously a very important piece of evidence in connection with the current debate about the rise of Israel.

If Israel was already such a force in Canaan in 1212 B.C.E., then Israel must have been established there for some time. Those who would like to push back the date for Israel's entry into Canaan, stress this aspect of the Merneptah Stele.

On the other hand, those who say that Israel's existence only begins with the monarchy have to deal with this troubling bit of evidence. I often wonder what would happen if we didn't have this fortuitously preserved find. I'm almost certain that those scholars who insist that Israel didn't exist before the monarchy and who tell us that there is no premonarchical history to be gleaned from the premonarchical accounts in the Bible would carry the day. The biblical tales we would convincingly be told are mere *bobbe-mysehs*, grandmothers' tales. How do these scholars deal with the Merneptah Stele, since it indubitably does exist. They say that Israel refers to something else. What that something else is, is not clear. I certainly can understand that the numbers in the Bible are exaggerated. And there is evidence even in the Bible that there were not always 12 tribes in a league together. But the Merneptah Stele does date from the time when the nation and people that became Israel were aborning, were in the early stages of their development.

A final point about the Merneptah Stele and its significance.

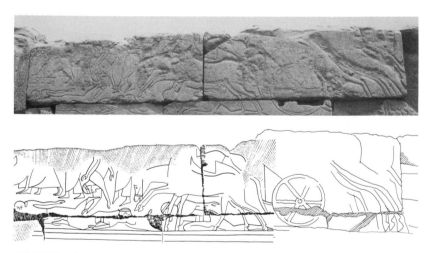

ILLUSTRATING THE MERNEPTAH STELE are recently identified reliefs from the Karnak temple at Thebes. But which panel portrays the Israelites? One scholar, Frank Yurco of the Field Museum in Chicago, believes that this panel (photo at top and drawing) illustrates the reference to Israel near the end of the stele. Significantly, the people depicted here as being subjugated by pharaoh's army wear ankle-length skirts identical to the skirts worn by others in scenes that unquestionably portray Canaanites. If Yurco's interpretation is correct, this relief is evidence for the view that the Israelites emerged out of Canaanite society.

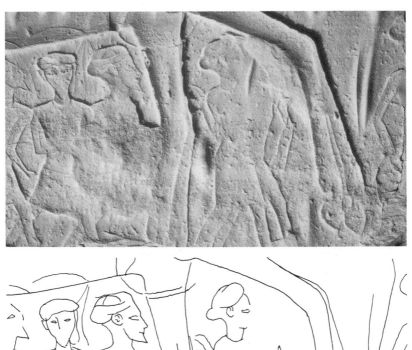

THESE *ARE THE ISRAELITES on the Karnak reliefs, counters Anson Rainey of Tel Aviv University. The reason that the people in the scene identified by Yurco as depicting Israel's destruction look like Canaanites is that they* are *Canaanites, says Rainey. Rainey believes that scene illustrates the first line of the Merneptah Stele's recap of the Canaanite campaign—"Canaan has been plundered into every sort of woe"—not the last line—"Israel is laid waste, his seed is not."*

In Rainey's analysis, the Israelites might be identified with the knee-length-skirted figures shown in the photo at top and drawing, the pastoralist people known as the Shasu, found elsewhere on the Karnak reliefs. Thus the Israelites would not have emerged from within Canaanite society at all, but may well have crystallized from wandering shepherds from outside Canaan.

Very recently, some reliefs on a temple at Karnak have been identified as illustrations of this famous passage from the Merneptah Stele.*
One panel of reliefs represents Ashkelon; other panels appear to
represent the other Canaanite cities mentioned in the Merneptah
Stele. Unfortunately, there is still a dispute as to which panel or
panels pictures the Israelites. In one panel that is a contender, the
Israelites have long togas or skirts, just like the other Canaanites. So
it is argued that this supports the contention that Israel emerged out
of Canaanite society. In another panel which supposedly represents
the Israelites, they have short skirts, quite unlike the Canaanites, so
this supports the argument that the Israelites entered Canaan from
outside the land.**

If they did come from outside the land, then this raises the
question of where they came from. In short, was there really an
Exodus? For the Exodus, we don't have a Merneptah Stele; we don't
have any evidence that the Israelites as such were in Egypt.

What we do have is evidence of Canaanite pottery in Egypt,
and we also have evidence that Canaanite traders would come down
to Egypt just like Jacob and his sons. A very famous picture from a
tomb at Beni Hasan in Egypt pictures some merchants from Asia
coming down to Egypt to do business. This tomb is beautifully
preserved in cliffs overlooking the Nile about halfway between Cairo
and Luxor.

Finally, there is evidence concerning a strange people known as
the Hyksos. That's the name by which we know them, but that's not
what they called themselves. The Hyksos were a people from Asia—
Canaan—who came down to Egypt and ultimately became the rulers of Egypt for two Egyptian dynasties. Ultimately, they were expelled by the Egyptians, who chased them back into Canaan. Obviously, the rise of the Hyksos in Egypt seems to have echoes in the
biblical story of Joseph. The expulsion of the Hyksos seems to be
some kind of Exodus in reverse. Instead of fleeing, they were kicked
out. Whether there is any connection between the Hyksos and the
biblical accounts I will leave to my good friend Baruch Halpern. In

---

* Frank J. Yurco, "3,200-Year-Old Picture of Israelites Found in Egypt," *Biblical Archaeology
Review,* September/October 1990.

** See also "Anson F. Rainey's Challenge," *Biblical Archaeology Review,* November/December
1991.

COLOR PLATE I

SEMITES IN EGYPT. Bearing the Egyptian title for Hyksos, a figure named Abisha (leaning over an ibex, second from right), leads his western Semitic clansmen into Egypt in order to conduct trade. The scene dates to about 1890 B.C.E. and has been preserved on the wall of one of the tombs carved into cliffs overlooking the Nile at Beni Hasan, about halfway between Cairo and Luxor.

"Hyksos" is a Greek term derived from an Egyptian phrase meaning either "ruler of foreign lands" or "shepherd-kings." The Hyksos were Canaanites who ruled Egypt for roughly two and a half centuries, starting about 1800 B.C.E.

COLOR PLATE II

LIKE THE BIBLICAL ISRAELITES, workmen labor at the task of making bricks in this wall painting from the tomb of the vizier Rekhmere. The details of Israelite slavery in the Bible mesh well with historical research: One Egyptian text bemoans the lack of straw for brickmaking (a detail also recorded by the Bible)—the fact that straw was used at all shows a familiarity with conditions in Egypt (straw was not typically used for making mudbrick in Canaan); the burdensome increase of forced labor under the pharaoh of the oppression may reflect the building boom under Ramesses II.

COLOR PLATE III
MERNEPTAH STELE. Discovered a century ago at Thebes, the 7.5-foot-high, hieroglyphic-covered black granite slab was commissioned by Pharaoh Merneptah during his fifth regnal year—1207 B.C.E.—to boast of his military successes in Libya. (For further information, see caption on page 18.)

COLOR PLATES IV and V

STANDING AT THE ALTAR? If Israeli archaeologist Adam Zertal is right, this nearly square (24.5 feet by 29.5 feet) stone structure (photo at top) on Mt. Ebal with what Zertal takes to be a 23-foot ramp leading up to it is the only instance of archaeological research bringing to life a specific instruction in the Hebrew Bible. Zertal believes this may be the altar described in Joshua 8:30-35 as the site of the recitation of the blessings and the curses following Israel's entry into Canaan. In the drawing, the altar and primary ramp are shown in yellow; blue highlights a lower ledge around three sides of the altar as well as a narrower and lower ramp alongside the main ramp. Other archaeologists disagree with Zertal's interpretation of the site, however, seeing it as nothing more than an isolated fort or a farmhouse.

COLOR PLATE VI

AGRICULTURAL TERRACES are cultivated today in much the same way as they were first utilized by the early Israelites more than 3,000 years ago. Stone retaining walls, stacked atop each other without mortar, lie at the outer edges of natural limestone terraces. The walls keep soil in place and create a level platform for farming; they also hamper water runoff, allowing the water to seep into the soil. The development of terraced farming facilitated the widespread habitation of the hill country.

the meantime, you can ask me a few questions, but not too many because what I have tried to do is simply give you a little background, some of the framework and parameters of the extraordinarily vigorous debates that are going on in the academy. From the other speakers, we are going to go out into the jungle. These are the people who are exploring beyond the point where I have taken you, developing the lines of thought that will dominate the discussion in the years to come.

ENDNOTES

1. See P. Kyle McCarter, Jr., "The Patriarchal Age," in *Ancient Israel: A Short History from Abraham to the Roman Destruction of the Temple*, ed. Hershel Shanks (Englewood Cliffs, NJ: Prentice-Hall; Washington, DC: Biblical Archaeology Society, 1988), pp. 1-29.

2. See Joseph A. Callaway, "The Settlement in Canaan," in Shanks, *Ancient Israel*, pp. 53-84.

Questions & Answers

Why do the houses that were found throughout the settlement area have to be early? And why can't they be people who lived away from the cities? And, how do you prove either statement?

Well, these people certainly did live away from large urban centers. There's no question about that. But where did they come from and who were they? They could have been, according to some theories, wandering pastoralists who decided to settle down. They could be Canaanites who were fleeing from the cities. It is possible to interpret much of the evidence in varying ways, and that is part of the problem. No mighty stream of evidence is developing and that's why I think we're still far from a consensus.

The Merneptah Stele records an Egyptian campaign in Canaan. I don't quite see the connection between that and the Israelite campaign to subject the Canaanites.

I'm sorry to have confused you. The Merneptah Stele is simply evidence of the existence of Israel at this time. The Egyptian campaign in Canaan we really don't know much about, but, in a sense, that is irrelevant to the issue of Israel's emergence in Canaan. The importance of the Merneptah Stele is that Israel unquestionably existed in Canaan in 1212 B.C.E. Second, Israel's presence in Canaan was of such importance that the pharoah knew about it. And third, one of the things in his reign that he was proudest of was that he claimed to have defeated Israel in this military campaign. I didn't intend to use that Egyptian campaign to demonstrate the Israelite conquest—only to demonstrate the existence of an important entity named Israel as a people, unlike the Canaanite cities also identified in the Merneptah Stele.

If the archaeological evidence does not support a conquest model, why would the Bible reflect a conquest model?

The purpose of the biblical account is not what we regard as history.

The purpose of the biblical account is to explain God's acts in relation to man on this earth. It really isn't concerned about detailed accuracy; that's not its purpose. Now, there is a certain divide among people who, on the one hand regard the Bible as literally true and, on the other, those who look at it as a document like any other ancient document: It has to be analyzed and compared and looked at for its *tendenz*, for its biases. My friend Bill Dever, has called the Bible "a curated artifact." There is a difference among people concerning how they approach the Bible. Those who accept the Bible as literally true are people who accept this on faith. I don't think we can argue on that ground. Other people say that, unlike those who accept the Bible as literally true, they will argue with you on archaeological or historical grounds. And it is in this area that you can have a debate. Most modern biblical scholars do not accept the Bible as literally true. So what you have to do is to treat it almost like an archaeological tell, and excavate it, as it were, and analyze it to see whether what it says is historically true in the details, whether we would accept it as historically accurate by modern historians' standards, by modern historiography. That is not to denigrate the richness of the biblical text. I think many people who do not accept the literal reading of the Bible find it a very enriching and inspiring and even Godly document, without the necessity of it being literally true in every detail. This whole discussion proceeds on the basis that we will examine the Bible in this way. What I have tried to do is to summarize some of the problems in the biblical text and to describe some of the ways scholars have dealt with them.

INTRODUCTION

I *have been accused of organizing this entire session solely to have the opportunity of introducing Bill Dever. (Laughter.) And I want to deny that. That's not the only reason. But it certainly is a pleasure for me to introduce an old friend with whom I have had some public disagreements. And I suppose for those of you who are aware of this, I should not simply gloss over them, but tell you that we are old and close friends despite our public professional disagreements. Basically, I think that is something that is over. It involved the use of the term "biblical archaeology." I thought it was a good and credible and continually viable term. Bill, at one point in his career, thought we ought to abandon it. The ironic thing is that throughout that period—and continuing—I don't know anyone who was a more insightful and perceptive biblical archaeologist than Bill Dever. (Laughter.) He confessed to me at dinner last night that he is getting less and less interested in his EBIV [Early Bronze IV period] business [pre-biblical] and turning more and more to the Bible. I was of course delighted to hear that.*

Bill Dever is one of the very few preeminent American, dare I say, biblical archaeologists. He directed for many years the ongoing excavations at Tel Gezer, which was a seminal excavation because it trained so many American archaeologists who are in the forefront today. He was for years the director of the American School of Oriental Research in Jerusalem, now the William F. Albright School of Archaeological Research. He's well on the way to completing the final report on the Gezer excavations. He has of course dug at many other sites— Shechem, Jebel Qa'aqir and Khirbet el-Kom. He brings a vast knowledge of inscriptions, as well as archaeological and biblical knowledge. He's an exciting lecturer. It is a pleasure for me to introduce my friend Bill Dever.—H.S.

WILLIAM G. DEVER

How to Tell a Canaanite from an Israelite

The reason why the debate is over is because I won. (Laughter.) There's nothing more to say.

But it's a pleasure to be here. I don't think I would have come this far except for two reasons: One, for Hershel Shanks; and two, for an audience as good as I knew this would be.

When Hershel and I first discussed this symposium, we talked about the topic being the emergence of Israel. Yet, when I got the program I noticed that I was talking about "how to tell an Israelite from a Canaanite"; that's Hershel's editorial flair. (Laughter.) I thought immediately of the biblical tradition. You remember that when the Israelites left Egypt, they went out into the wilderness where they longed for the leeks and the onions they had enjoyed in Egypt. So I thought perhaps we could smell their breath. (Laughter.) But both the Canaanites and the Israelites have been gone for 2,500 years, so that won't work.

The question, however, is legitimate. That is: Who were the

Israelites and where did they come from—geographically, socially and ideologically? How did the Israelites differ from their Canaanite neighbors? What, if anything, was unique about ancient Israel?

I have tried to wrestle with these questions as an archaeologist. I want to say just a word, however, before we look at the newer archaeological evidence—a word about the limitations of our sources, both literary and archaeological. Today we have two brilliant expositions regarding the Bible as a source for history-writing. Both remind us of the limitations of the biblical text as a historical source. The word "history" does not even occur in the Hebrew Bible. The Bible is not history; it doesn't pretend to be. It is literature, and a peculiar brand of *theological* literature at that. It is a reconstruction of the past after the past was essentially over; written, edited and put together in its present form long after the collapse of both the northern kingdom (Israel) and the southern kingdom (Judah). It therefore refracts, as well as reflects, the past. The Bible is a kind of revisionist history.

One of my theological colleagues likes to remind me that the Bible is a "minority report." It was written by the ultra-right-wing orthodox party after the fall of Israel (the northern kingdom to the Assyrians and the southern kingdom to the Babylonians) to explain the tragedy of those events. The biblical writers are not telling it the way it was, but the way it would have been had they been in charge. (Laughter.) And that obviously gives us a rather skewed view of Israel's past.

Until recently, the only source we had was the Bible, that is, before the birth of modern archaeology. For many people that was enough. The Bible seems very simple—if you are a bit simple-minded in your approach. I saw a bumper sticker in Tucson recently that declared, "God said it, I believe it and that settles it." (Laughter.) But of course it doesn't; at least it doesn't for those who have inquiring minds.

Archaeology won't settle the matter either. But what archaeology does do is provide a fresh perspective. Thus it solves some problems, but creates others. Archaeology produces what William Foxwell Albright, the dean of American biblical archaeology, called "external data." If the data in the allegedly historical sources in the Hebrew Bible are somewhat limited, archaeology provides us with a never-

WILLIAM FOXWELL ALBRIGHT (1891-1971), the late doyen of American biblical archaeology. Albright described archaeology, in contrast to the biblical account, as a source of "external data" free from the biases of ancient authors and editors. But even such unalloyed data, warns William Dever, can become tainted as soon as archaeologists begin to introduce their own interpretations of them. Albright himself is a good case in point, says Dever. While his reputation remains unsurpassed, Albright's defense of the conquest model for Israel's emergence in Israel is now largely discredited.

ending supply of *new* data that come without the editorial biases of the ancient authors and redactors. (The archaeological data are unbiased, however, only until we begin to interpret them, and then we introduce our own biases.) Potentially archaeology is a very exciting source of new information about the Bible and the biblical world.

I propose first to say a word about the two or three models of Israel's emergence in Canaan that have already been mentioned. Then I want to show you quite a lot of archaeological data, and at the end I'll try to give some answers.

The models were discussed by Hershel. (You will forgive us if we all call each other by our first names. We are in fact old friends. But of course that doesn't mean that we agree about everything.) The conquest model is not subscribed to by most biblical scholars today—certainly no one in the mainstream of scholarship—and that's been true for some time. Moreover, there isn't a single reputable professional archaeologist in the world who espouses the conquest model in Israel, Europe or America. We don't need to say any more about the conquest model. That's that. (Laughter.) Not to be dogmatic about it or anything, but . . . (Laughter.)

Moving to the second model, the peaceful infiltration model; that seems all right until you try to chase pastoral nomads around. They don't leave many traces in the archaeological record. You can talk about movements of people from Transjordan, going across the Jordan River into western Palestine; but there is, in fact, almost no archaeological evidence to support such movements. It's an intriguing model—and I will suggest a version of it myself—but archaeologically it's very hard to use. I suspect that the peaceful infiltration model rests on a kind of 19th-century nostalgia about the Bedouin, and also on ignorance about pastoral nomads and how they really operate. Many of the theories about [the emergence of] Israel as derived from pastoral nomadic origins are now suspect; they rest on faulty archaeology and faulty biblical scholarship.

If we turn to the so-called peasant revolt model, the peasants may indeed have been revolting, but that's not the point. Again, this is a 20th-century construct. The biblical account of Israel's origins is also a construct. So the peasant revolt model is a construct forced back upon what was already a construct. It reflects a Marxist rhetoric (and who would want to be Marxist today?). As an archaeologist, there is very little I can say about the peasant revolt model, because it rests on ideological assumptions that are very difficult to test archaeologically. What I like about it is that it stresses the indigenous origins of most early Israelites. And that does fit the archaeological evidence. But whether the early Israelites were "Yahwists" is almost impossible to say from the viewpoint of the archaeological data. (I will reflect upon that at the end of my talk.)

A fourth model was not mentioned, but it has been advanced recently by a German scholar, Volkmar Fritz, and it is one I tend to agree with. It's called the symbiosis model. It suggests that the people I will call "proto-Israelites," or earliest Israelites, lived for a rather long period of time alongside the Canaanites—not all the Israelites perhaps, but the majority of them. And they emerged in some way out of Late Bronze Age urban Canaanite society. That is the picture that the archaeological evidence supports better.

Let's look at the new evidence.[1] Much of this was not available even ten years ago, and a large part of it is still not published. But it represents a growing body of knowledge about which I think we can be fairly confident. I know we all stress the controversies amongst scholars, and they are very real indeed because scholars have rather healthy egos. But, in fact, there is a growing scholarly consensus on this matter. At the end I want to stress the points on which I think we probably all will agree. It's a very different picture from the one we would have painted just ten or fifteen years ago. That is what's exciting about archaeology. The biblical text is what it is, it cannot change; only our interpretation of it changes. But archaeology changes every day. If you invite me back next year I'll tell you a different story; but at the moment this is the best that we have—or at least that I have.

As background to the archaeological presentation, however, let me reiterate that the traditional notion of Moses receiving the Law at Sinai is not a story that we can comment on archaeologically. I do think—as Baruch Halpern brilliantly suggests—that behind the literary tradition there must indeed be some sort of genuine historical memory; but it is unfortunately not accessible either to the text scholar or to the archaeologist. If we consider the biblical description of the Tabernacle in the wilderness, for instance, we can say nothing about its historicity. Once in awhile you hear reports that somebody has found, or is planning to find, the Ark of the Covenant. (Laughter.) A man came into my office recently and suggested that the Israelis actually know where it is. It is made of gold, and it is hidden in a cave near Bethlehem. If we could just raise money, and if I would get him a permit to dig, we could find it and make ourselves rich and famous. I suggested another place where he might go . . . (Laughter.) As far as I know the Ark has not been found, and I wouldn't go looking for it. (Laughter.)

According to the biblical tradition, the people who later formed Israel entered the country through the backdoor, from the east via Jericho. Gradually they fanned out northward and southward, and in a very short time they overran the land, virtually annihilating the native population of Canaan, then apportioning all of the territories amongst the 12 tribes. Now we know at least something about many archaeological sites on both sides of the Jordan river. At Hazor in upper Galilee, where the late Yigael Yadin excavated, he believed that he had found evidence of the Israelite destruction; and, as you know, the site figures prominently in the Joshua tradition (Joshua 11:1-15). The Israelites are said to have killed Jabin the king of Hazor, "the head of all those kingdoms" (Joshua 11:10). Today, however, most archaeologists are inclined to date this destruction about 1250 B.C.E., probably too early for the Israelites, at least under Joshua.

At the site of Lachish in the south, an earlier dig dated a destruction level to about 1220 B.C.E., which would fit the Joshua account. But recently scarabs of the later Ramesside pharaohs have been found that require us to bring that destruction level down to about 1150 B.C.E. or a little later. Now, clearly it is not possible for Joshua to have led the Israelite troops against Hazor in 1250 B.C.E. and against Lachish in 1150 B.C.E.—unless he was carried out onto the battlefield on a stretcher. Neither of these destructions can be attributed with confidence to the Israelites.

Let me put the matter categorically. There is not a single de-struction layer around 1200 B.C.E. that we can ascribe with certainty to the Israelites. There are some possible Israelite destructions; there are none, however, that are certain. Many sites, like Jericho and Ai (and others), were not even occupied in this period. In Transjordan, the same is true; sites like Hesbon (biblical Heshbon), Dibhan (bibli-cal Dibon) and others that are mentioned in the biblical accounts were not occupied in the late 13th or early 12th century B.C.E., so they cannot have been destroyed. Archaeology can rarely prove some-thing in the affirmative, but it can often prove things in the negative. It can prove that such and such did not happen, and could not have happened. That's the case here, because the archaeological record is totally silent.

The site of Shiloh has recently been excavated by the Israeli archaeologist Israel Finkelstein. In the biblical tradition, Shiloh was the tribal center where the Ark was kept (1 Samuel 1). But despite the most determined search, Israeli archaeologists have not been able to find anything of the Tabernacle or the shrine—or indeed anything cultic at all—from the 12th century B.C.E. And although the site was occupied earlier by the Canaanites, there is no evidence of any destruction. The site was simply taken over in the 12th cen-tury, perhaps by new peoples.

There are possibly two early Israelite shrines that do belong to the late 13th or 12th century B.C.E. The first is the Mt. Ebal installa-tion near Shechem (modern Nablus on the West Bank), excavated by Adam Zertal.[2] This structure dates mostly to the 12th century B.C.E., and it has been argued that this is the very shrine described in the accounts in Joshua 8:30-35. The date is acceptable, since an Egyptian scarab found there can be dated to the late 13th century B.C.E. But there are reasons to doubt that the Mt. Ebal installation is a shrine at all. Occupation levels produced burned bones of four kinds of animals, three of them mentioned in the Hebrew Bible in connection with descriptions of sacrificial rituals. Sheep, goats and small cattle are indeed kosher, but roe deer are not. Zertal has reconstructed the installation as a large outdoor altar upon which animal sacrifices were made, connecting it directly with the Bible. If he is correct, this is the only instance in which archaeology has ever brought to life a specific installation described in the Hebrew Bible. It would be wonderful if it were true, but it's probably not. Most Israeli archaeologists think the Mt. Ebal installation is an isolated fort or a farmhouse. I have my own interpretation. Judging from the splendid

A CARNELIAN SCARAB discovered at the Mt. Ebal installation helps to provide a date for the site. Issued during the reign of Ramesses II (1279-1213 B.C.E.) to honor Thutmosis III (1479-1425 B.C.E.), the scarab features a large figure at center that looks like a capital B; the shape is actually a double bow held by a kneeling archer at far left. The area to the right of the B—called a cartouche—contains Thutmosis III's name. A second scarab from the site also dates to Ramesses II. Zertal's claim that the Mt. Ebal installation is an altar from the time of Joshua is disputed by some archaeologists and supported by others.

vistas from the hilltop, the lovely breeze you get up on the mountain and the evidence of all the burned animal bones, I think it's a picnic site where barbecues were enjoyed by families on Saturday afternoons. (Laughter.)

The second site, however, has a better pedigree—the so-called bull site, excavated by Amihai Mazar, one of the leading younger archaeologists in Israel today.[3] It lies near biblical Dothan, north of Shechem in the hill country of Samaria. It is a small, isolated hilltop shrine with very few remains, clearly not a domestic site. It belongs to the 12th century B.C.E. to judge from the pottery fragments. The

THE HAZOR BULL. Strikingly similar to the figurine found near Dothan in Samaria (color photo, see cover), this bronze bull from Hazor dates to the 14th century B.C.E.— making it a clearly Canaanite object. In the Canaanite pantheon the chief god was called El, and his principal epithet was "Bull El."

stones around it make up a kind of enclosure, or *temenos* wall. Mazar found a cobbled area and what the Hebrew Bible calls a *massebah*, or standing stone, of some sort. Here I think that the cultic interpretation is sound. The site is in the heartland of the ancient tribal territory of Ephraim, and we can probably ascribe it to Israelite settlers. The prize find from the site, found before Mazar excavated it, is a splendidly preserved bronze bull about 4 inches high (see cover). A similar bronze bull was found at Hazor, but from the 14th century, clearly Canaanite. In the Canaanite pantheon the chief god was called El, and his principal epithet was "Bull El." His consort was Asherah, the great mother goddess of Canaan. The point is that at perhaps the only Israelite shrine we have from the 12th century B.C.E., the chief totem animal is almost identical to the old Canaanite bull deity El.

We have almost no other evidence for religion. In short, Yahwism, with all its attendant institutions and traditions, was no doubt a product of a later period, as I think Professor McCarter will show you in the last talk. We have very little archaeological evidence in the 12th or 11th century B.C.E. of early Israelite religious beliefs or practice. That is not to say that they did not exist, but they are not very accessible to the archaeologist.

Next I want to consider the early Israelite settlement sites. It was mentioned earlier today that we know of over 200 settlement sites from the 12th and 11th centuries B.C.E. in the central hill country. In fact, we now have over 300 that we might connect with the earliest penetration of the Israelites into the hill country (see map, p. 11).

I want to look at two such sites near Jerusalem. One is Ai, to the northeast of Jerusalem, and the other is Raddana, very near Ai. Ai is, of course, a major biblical site; it figures prominently in the conquest narratives in Joshua 7-8. Yet a staunch American Southern Baptist archaeologist, Joe Callaway, excavated there for many years, quite anxious to prove the biblical tradition, but unable to come up with anything at all. The site was not even occupied in the 13th century B.C.E., so it cannot have been destroyed by the Israelites. Ai's story is thus very much like the story of Jericho.* For the true

---

* On Ai, see Joseph Callaway, "A Visit with Ahilud," *Biblical Archaeology Review*, September/October 1983. See also Callaway, "Was My Excavation of Ai Worthwhile?" *Biblical Archaeology Review*, March/April 1988.

believer, however, this kind of factual evidence is not a problem, not any barrier to belief at all. After all, if Joshua destroyed a site that wasn't even there, that's a stupendous miracle—even better than the one described in the Bible. (Laughter.) So, if you want to believe the story, you're welcome to do so, but there's no archaeological evidence to help you.

At nearby Raddana, on the outskirts of modern Ramalleh, there was a salvage dig, also led by Callaway. It brought to light the re-

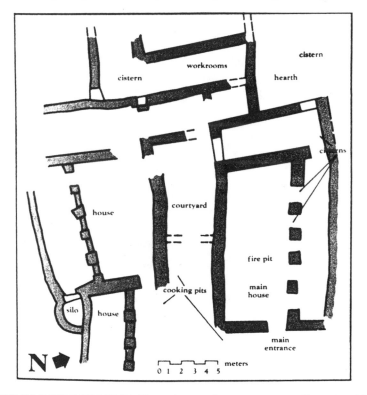

EARLY ISRAELITE HOUSING. The 12th- or 11th-century B.C.E. village of Raddana, about ten miles north of Jerusalem, contains well-preserved examples of pillared courtyard houses. Behind the workman in the photo at right is the largest room of the main house (lower right in the drawing); four pillars at far right separate it from a long narrow room farther to the right. The pillars probably supported a second story where the inhabitants lived and slept; the ground floor may have served as stables for animals. The central courtyard, around which stood two additional houses for the extended family, contained pits for cooking. The courtyard house is a pervasive feature of Canaanite hill-country sites and is almost certainly the type of structure referred to in the Bible by the phrase "the house of the father" (Hebrew: bet av).

mains of a 12th- or 11th-century B.C.E. village. The modern name is Khirbet Raddana, but many people believe that the site may be identified with ancient El-Bireh, known from biblical tradition.[4]

Raddana contained some nicely preserved examples of courtyard houses, or pillared courtyard houses as I prefer to call them, sometimes regarded as "early Israelite" houses. On either side of a central pillared courtyard were roofed and cobbled areas where animals were stabled. There were also large areas for storing both dry and liquid foodstuffs. Cisterns were dug under the floors of the houses and in the courtyards to provide a ready source of water. In fact, one of the reasons that the area was never effectively settled before the Iron Age was that the art of digging cisterns had not yet been perfected, and you cannot survive in the hill country in the summertime without some means of water catchment. In the central courtyard was also a firepit. On the second floor of the house, you would have had the living and sleeping quarters.

This same type of courtyard house appears again and again at each of these hill-country sites. Today the hills where these settlements were built are barren and largely abandoned. But archaeologists have found evidence of intensive terracing of the hillsides in the past. That, too, was a new technology, perfected in the late 13th and early 12th centuries B.C.E. Without that, one could not have farmed the rugged, steep hills of central Palestine. Terraces, formed by stone walls, not only get rid of the rocks covering the ground but they create a kind of stepped platform on which a donkey or an ox can pull a plow. And of course the terraces impeded runoff rain in the winter, allowing the water to percolate down. Thus terraces were a very clever device for exploiting the hill-country frontier, which had never been intensively settled before the late 13th and early 12th centuries. These terraces, one of the most important innovations of these newcomers, are a clue to their origin. (Of this, more later.)

At all of the hill-country sites, when a new house was built, it often shared a common courtyard with the older house, and even the main walls. In a brilliant article, Lawrence Stager has shown that the plan and layout of these houses, as well as that of the overall villages, could have come straight out of the pages of the Book of Judges.[5]

Now archaeologists are not very fond of the Book of Joshua,

for reasons about which we've spoken. The Book of Judges, on the other hand, has the ring of truth about it, at least from what we know given the facts on the ground. In Judges, Samuel and Kings, and even in Joshua, when an Israelite identifies himself as a *gever*, or individual, he will say typically that he belongs to the house of X, "the house of the father" (Hebrew, *bet av*). As Stager has noted, that almost certainly is the compound house unit in which an extended family lived. In biblical times, as in modern times in the West Bank and elsewhere in the Middle East, when a young man marries he brings his bride to his father's house and she joins the family. At the same time, an older couple, the grandparents, may be living there. So you tend to get an "extended family," often three generations and as many as 20 individuals living together. Therefore, in the typical layout of these hill-country villages, what you are seeing is in fact a

THE VIEW INSIDE A CISTERN. The cap on this household cistern, part of an interconnected series of cisterns at Ai, was set in place during Iron Age I (1200-1000 B.C.E.) and remained undisturbed until excavations in the 1960s. Cisterns cut into bedrock such as this are typically bell-shaped (see drawing). The development of iron tools to dig such pits and the introduction of terraced farming (see color plate VI) are two technological innovations that facilitated the settlement of the proto-Israelites in the central hill country of Canaan.

cluster of individual houses, the biblical *bet av*. The entire village—comprising perhaps a dozen such compounds—would then comprise the biblical *mishpachah*, not simply "family," but "kinship group," since everyone was related, as in Middle Eastern villages today. Stager has thus shown how in the very buildings themselves and in their furnishings we can see actual terms used in the Hebrew Bible for their socioeconomic structure. Stager's analysis is one of the most successful articles yet in the field of biblical archaeology. Biblical archaeology may not exist, but Stager has done it brilliantly. (Laughter.)

Here in these hill-country villages, for the first time we find the early Israelites in actual archaeological context. We ought not to be chasing around Palestine looking at the great mounds and trying to dig ash layers that we can connect with destruction stories in the Bible. Instead, we ought to be looking at social and economic history, at how the new sites—both excavated and identified in surveys—may reflect the very terminology of the Hebrew Bible. That suggests that there is something behind these stories, even though they could not have been written down before the tenth century B.C.E. There is no doubt that there is some genuine historical experience reflected in these stories. (More on that later.)

The common early Israelite pottery turns out to be nearly identical to that of the late 13th century B.C.E.; it comes right out of the Late Bronze Age urban Canaanite repertoire. As someone who has spent 30 years studying this pottery, I can tell you that, based on the pottery evidence, we would not even suspect that the people living in these hill-country sites were newcomers at all. One can't imagine nomads sweeping in from the desert, with no architectural or ceramic tradition behind them, suddenly becoming past masters of the potter's art in Palestine. This early Iron Age I (c. 1200 B.C.E.) pottery goes back eight or ten centuries in a long Middle–Late Bronze Age tradition. Clearly the pottery alone suggests that these newcomers to the hill country were not newcomers to Palestine. They had been living alongside the Canaanite city-states for some time, perhaps for several generations, probably for several centuries.[6]

By the way, I must tell you that the early Israelite pottery is pretty drab, while the Philistine painted pottery is quite sophisticated. In a wonderful twist of historical irony, we remember the

Philistines as barbarians. But that is a value judgment from the Judeo-Christian perspective. I'm afraid it's the early Israelites who were the barbarians when it comes to making pottery. Perhaps they already had their minds on spiritual things. But the pottery is terrible stuff. We know *what* it is, however. It comes out of the local Canaanite repertoire. There is nothing Transjordanian about it, and certainly nothing Egyptian about it. There's nothing much new in it either, apart from the normal and even predictable ceramic developments.

In several sites we have evidence for a kind of cottage industry in metallurgy. We find a lot of copper and bronze, but not much iron, which suggests that iron was not yet an important factor, even in the early Iron Age. We don't get many iron implements before the

CONTRARY TO THEIR REPUTATION AS BARBARIANS, the Philistines produced sophisticated painted pottery at a time when their Israelite contemporaries were still generating undistinguished pots straight out of the Canaanite repertoire. The Philistines were one of the Sea Peoples, Aegean seafarers who settled along the Canaanite coast in about 1175 B.C. When they first settled in their new homeland, the Philistines produced pottery made of local clays but fashioned in Mycenaean style. Known as monochrome pottery, this ceramic ware was decorated in either black or red. In the latter half of the 12th century B.C.E., the Philistines began producing the type of pottery shown here, called bichrome ware. As the name indicates, such pottery is decorated in two colors, red and black. The bowls and pitchers in the photo bear typical Philistine ornamentations, most notably the bird at far right.

tenth century, at about the time of the formation of the Israelite state. In the early period, the so-called period of the Judges, we get not only copper and bronze implements but even some stone tools.

The picture we get in these early Israelite hill-country villages is of a very simple, rather impoverished, somewhat isolated culture with no great artistic or architectural tradition behind it. And yet one does not get the notion that these people were simply pastoral nomads in the process of becoming sedentarized. For instance, in these early settlements we have some indications of literacy. Archaeologists have rather large imaginations; we find one jar handle with

AN EARLY SIGN OF ISRAELITE LITERACY? This inscribed jar handle from Raddana, dating to the late 13th or early 12th century, bears (from top to bottom) the letters aleph (a), het (h) and lamed (l). Adding the letter dalet completes the name Ahilud, a name known from contemporaneous references in 2 Samuel 8:16 and 20:24. William Dever points out that the writing on this handle is in Canaanite alphabetic script—a strong indication that the early Israelites were culturally indistinct from the Canaanites.

three inscribed letters, and already "It's a literate society." But the point is that if somebody could write, then a lot of people could write. And we are speaking not of the old, cumbersome cuneiform script or the Egyptian hieroglyphic script. What we have is the local Canaanite alphabetic script. At Raddana a jar handle was found with an inscription on it from the late 13th or early 12th century. Restoring one missing letter, we can read, "Belonging to Ahilud." That turns out to be a biblical name. Even though we have only hints of writing, clearly there is the beginning of a literate tradition in the earliest years of these proto-Israelite settlements.

Typically these villages are not founded on the ruins of destroyed Late Bronze Age urban Canaanite sites. They are established *de novo*, mostly on small, isolated hilltops. Most of the sites were undefended, with no city wall. And they were very small, not more than three or four of those big multiple-house compounds of which we spoke. The total population of most of these 300 or so villages was probably under 100; the largest that we know of cannot have been much over 300. If you combine these 300 or so sites and multiply by the numbers of houses and the area enclosed, the total population of early Israelites was perhaps about 75,000 for the entire central hill country north and south of Jerusalem, as well as the mountains of Lower Galilee. So we cannot think in terms of the inflated figures given in the biblical tradition, which are impossible. As Baruch [Halpern] will tell you, it is impossible for three million Israelites to have survived in the Negev desert, and in any case we cannot actually account for more than a population of 75,000 or so in the 12th century B.C.E. when the Israelite settlers appear in Palestine. By the 11th century, however, that population had doubled, and that is, I think, quite significant.

Now let's look at the kind of pottery vessels Hershel said are connected with these sites—the so-called collared-rim store jars (see photo, p. 10). The rim at the top is not just decorative, it's also functional, a way of strengthening the neck of the jar. Bear in mind that these are big jars, some of them standing 3 feet high or more. You do not find them in the urban Canaanite city-states. This is perhaps the only form of new pottery that you find in the so-called Israelite settlements. Why? The answer is simple. These are ideal vessels for storage of the agricultural surpluses that you must have to survive in these villages. They are practical vessels, typical of rural areas. So the differences in pottery at Canaanite and Israelite sites may not be ethnic differences at all, and they are certainly not chronological differences. What we see is a *functional* difference—the difference between the pottery repertoire typical of urban sites, and that of rural sites. Here we are clearly dealing with rural sites. The point has been made by Hershel and others that these storage jars are occasionally found in earlier periods. They are also found in parts of Transjordan that probably were not claimed by early Israel. This therefore is *not* an Israelite-type vessel, as sometimes stated. It is simply a very practical kind of jar for the kind of settlements we have been talking about in the hill country.

Let's look now at the site of 'Izbet Sartah, excavated by Israel Finkelstein[7] (see photo, p. 9). It's near the site of Aphek, a large Canaanite city-state that was partially destroyed a little before 1200 B.C.E. I am bold enough to suggest that this site is ancient Ebenezer. You remember the biblical story of the Ark being captured here by the Philistines (1 Samuel 4:1-18). If you know the site, you can almost see the battle. The Israelites had pressed down close to the coastal plain, but they were still living within the shadow of a large Canaanite town. This area is a buffer zone, on the natural border between the Philistine plain and the hill country where the new proto-Israelite sites were being settled. There are three strata at 'Izbet Sartah, covering the 12th to the mid-10th century B.C.E. The lowest stratum (III), according to Finkelstein, had a circle of houses. From this, he argues that the inhabitants were pastoral nomads settling down. In other words, these houses were arranged in the same way that Bedouin sometimes arrange their tents in a circle or an oval, or in the way that wagons would be gathered in a circle when the American West was being explored and settled. That's an interesting theory—and almost certainly wrong! Finkelstein's own field director, Zvi Lederman, has argued that in fact there was no such circle of houses. You can see for yourself in Finkelstein's own plan where he shows in black the areas that were actually excavated; the white areas are reconstructions by the archaeologist. Here, however, the archaeologist has ignored his own data. Finkelstein argues that the pottery from the earliest stratum can be identified as early Israelite and is totally different from the Late Bronze Age Canaanite repertoire.

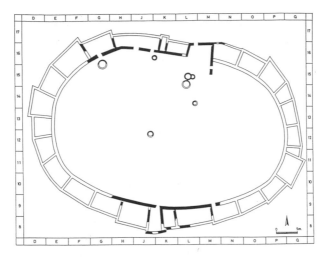

DRAWING THE WAGONS INTO A CIRCLE. The plan shows excavated areas of 'Izbet Sartah stratum III (late 13th century to the first half of the 11th century B.C.E.) in black; white represents structures conjectured by archaeologist Israel Finkelstein to have been present at the time. Finkelstein believes that the settlement's houses were built in a circle, much the way the Bedouin arrange their tents when encamping or—to stretch the analogy—the way pioneers on the American frontier circled their wagons for protection against marauders. In Finkelstein's view, the inhabitants of 'Izbet Sartah stratum III were pastoral nomads in the process of settling down. He identifies these people as early Israelites, distinguishable from their Canaanite neighbors by their architecture and by their pottery.

William Dever argues that the late 13th century B.C.E. buildings at 'Izbet Sartah stratum III may not have been arranged in circular fashion because not enough survived to justify Finkelstein's reconstruction. Dever sees little basic difference in the material evidence between the people at this site and the undoubted Canaanites at nearby Gezer.

Now I spent 25 years excavating at Gezer, which is only eight miles away from 'Izbet Sartah, and I've handled thousands of pieces of this pottery. The pottery from 'Izbet Sartah is *identical* to the pottery we found at Gezer. Now no one says that 12th-century Gezer was an Israelite site; on the contrary, it was without question a Canaanite site. It was not destroyed at the end of the Late Bronze Age, and remained a large urban site right through the Iron I period. Yet the pottery from Gezer and 'Izbet Sartah could have been made by the same potter. There is very little difference indeed. If the people at 'Izbet Sartah were Israelites, they were clearly using Canaanite-style pottery.

Finkelstein must know this, so he draws an analogy with modern pastoral nomads and argues that ancient pastoral nomads (his "Israelites") absorbed Canaanite ceramic traditions over a period of time, just as Bedouin or pastoral nomads do when they settle down and become farmers. He does not argue that the newcomers came from Transjordan, much less from Egypt. He believes that they had been present in Palestine from earliest times. The Israelites, then, are simply local pastoral nomads in the process of settling down. No one denies that pastoral nomads do become sedentarized. But I would argue that these proto-Israelites for the most part were probably not pastoral nomads at all. (More on this later.)

In the next stratum at 'Izbet Sartah (II), we see a real change in architecture. Here we have the same courtyard house that Hershel showed you (see plan, p. 8, photo, p. 9). In this stratum, the archaeologists found well-preserved seeds and bone samples, indicating to me that these people were experienced stockbreeders. They were efficient farmers, able to produce quite large surpluses. What did they do with their surpluses? They put them in the silos and storage pits that were found all over the site, typical of all the hill-country sites. These are isolated farming villages, which don't trade with the cities, so they must store agricultural surpluses.

Incidentally, this same kind of courtyard house continued to be used right down to the end of Israelite and Judahite history in the sixth century B.C.E. This is the Israelite-type house later on. The continuity in domestic house types is one thing that leads me to believe that these proto-Israelites were the authentic ancestors of the later Israelites of the Hebrew Bible. That is one of the reasons I use the label "Israelite" for them. The *continuity of material culture* from the tenth through the sixth century B.C.E. is clear. If people from places like 'Izbet Sartah were not Israelites, then those who were citizens of the later state were not Israelites either.

In one of the pits at 'Izbet Sartah there was found a broken piece of pottery with an inscription scratched into it. The inscription is what is called an abecedary—an alphabet. It was probably written by a schoolboy as a practice text. It probably dates from a little before 1100 B.C.E. Obviously, if people were practicing the alphabet at that time, they could write. But there are some interesting features here. Hebrew was written later from right to left, but this fellow

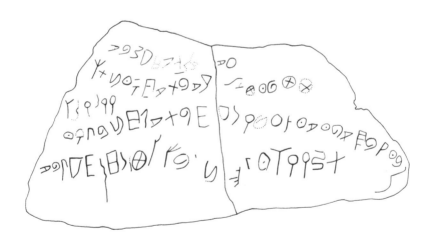

HOMEWORK FROM THE IRON AGE. Shortly before 1100 B.C.E., someone at 'Izbet Sartah, perhaps a schoolchild learning to write, inscribed letters of the alphabet on a pottery fragment (photo at top and drawing). Fragments such as this one are known as an abecedary; on this example the last line contains an almost complete proto-Hebrew alphabet. Curiously this alphabet reads from left to right, contrary to later Hebrew. Most importantly the script is Canaanite, leading William Dever to conclude that the early Israelites were at this time still writing and speaking a language indistinguishable from the Canaanites. Hebrew as a national tongue and script was not to emerge until the establishment of the monarchy in the tenth century B.C.E.

hadn't quite gotten it down yet. So he wrote it from left to right. He also got a few letters out of place, and some of them have the wrong stance. Altogether, it's a fairly crude exercise, but there's no doubt what we have. It's an abecedary, and the script is Canaanite. So again these early Israelites, whoever they were, were writing in a Canaanite script and probably speaking a dialect that was still a subdialect of Canaanite. Hebrew had not yet emerged as a national language and script, a development that came only with the establishment of the monarchy in the tenth century.

Many of the sites we have been talking about were abandoned in the tenth century B.C.E., toward the beginning of the monarchy. With the beginning of urbanization in ancient Israel, these rural sites were no longer viable. Many were never occupied again and thus did not build up into large mounds, and for that reason they were not even discovered until the last ten or fifteen years. They are especially valuable archaeological sites, however, because they were not built over by later people, and the material is just below the surface. Unfortunately, they are being rapidly destroyed by modern development. Furthermore, the survey work the Israelis were able to do just five years ago in the West Bank could not be done today because of political tensions. But the point is that in the physical remains of these hill-country sites there is reflected the kind of social and economic structure that comes right out of the pages of the Book of Judges. You couldn't have a better example of biblical archaeology of the right type.

I also want to mention the site of Tel Masos from this same period, where the paleoethnozoologist analyzed the animal bones and found that more than 65 percent of them were cattle bones—not sheep and goats.[8] These people were not shepherds settling down; they were experienced stockbreeders. They were not country bumpkins either, since the pottery shows trade contact with urban sites on the coast. Now Finkelstein argues that Tel Masos is not Israelite. Why? Because it doesn't fit his model! But not even the Bible suggests that all Israelite sites were alike. Masos is different in some ways. Some of the Masos houses are larger than others, but there is no monumental architecture at all. There are no palaces, no city walls or gates, no temples.

Indeed, none have been found in any of these proto-Israelite settlements. That's what has led some scholars like Norman Gottwald to suggest that what we have in these settlements is a kind of primitive democracy, or egalitarian society. That's stretching it a bit, I think; no known society is completely unstratified. Nevertheless, it is clear that Masos, like the other sites, is not yet urbanized. There are no specialized "elites" in any of these sites; there is a kind of homogeneity to the material culture. You recall what is said in the Book of Judges—that "In those days there was no king in Israel, and every man did what was right in his own eyes" (Judges 21:25). (What the women did, we don't know. Laughter.) Masos, along with about a half dozen of the 300 known sites, has been excavated—none with a very large exposure. What we have are intensive surface surveys over the last 15 years that have absolutely revolutionized our knowledge of Iron I settlements in the hill country.

Now let's look at some percentages. At the end of the Late Bronze Age, in the 13th century B.C.E., in the whole of the hill country west of the Jordan we know of only about 25 sites. In Iron I, however, we have more than 250 sites. There has been an enormous increase in population that cannot be accounted for by natural birthrates alone. Vast numbers of new people were indeed moving into the hill country in the 12th century B.C.E. And the movement crested in the 11th century, when the population probably doubled. This is a fascinating demographic portrait, one of which we had no idea just 15 years ago.

What do the demographics mean? That's the really intriguing question. Adam Zertal claims that he has identified three types of cooking pots. One flourished in the late 13th and early 12th century, right around 1200 B.C.E. Another slightly different cooking pot flourished in the mid- to late-12th century B.C.E. A third kind of cooking pot appeared in the 11th century B.C.E. No one doubts the dates of these respective cooking pots, but Zertal's interpretation of them is suspect. He has picked up fragments of these cooking pots in a survey of 136 sites in the area allotted to the tribe of Manasseh, now in the West Bank.* He argues, in essence, that the sites with the *earliest* cooking pots are on the eastern slopes of the central ridge, nearer the Jordan Valley. The later ones are found toward the central

---

* On Zertal's Manasseh survey, see "Israel Enters Canaan—Following the Pottery Trail," *Biblical Archaeology Review*, September/October 1991.

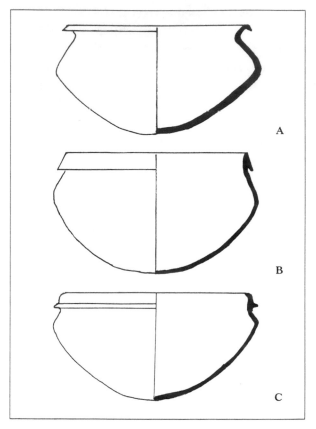

A

B

C

SMALL CHANGES, IMPORTANT RAMIFICATIONS. *The drawing charts a subtle evolution in pottery styles that bolsters, some archaeologists believe, the theory that the Israelites entered Canaan from Transjordan, settled first in the eastern Canaanite hill country and then migrated west. The left half of each drawing shows the intact vessel as seen from outside; the right half shows the pot as if it had been sliced vertically, with the width of the wall indicated in thick black. The first type of vessel (top), common during the late 13th and early 12th century B.C.E., is marked by an everted triangular rim. The middle pot, which flourished in the mid- to late-12th century, features a less pointy, tongued rim. The third type, appearing in the 11th century, bears a long tongue on the rim.*

Adam Zertal believes that the earliest type of pottery is more common in the eastern Canaanite hill country and that the later types are more common in the central and western sections of the highlands. Zertal sees this as evidence of Israelite migration. William Dever counters that even according to Zertal's own findings, no such movement can be attributed to the pottery record. If any early pottery types—even if they were not the dominant style—were present at a site, Dever emphasizes, that site must have been settled during the earlier period. A straightforward east-to-west migration theory, Dever says, is therefore no longer tenable.

hill country and westward. For Zertal that means that there was a movement of newcomers arriving from the east and moving westward. Where did they come from in the east? Why, from Transjordan, of course.

As far as I'm concerned, Zertal's theory cannot be demonstrated archaeologically. It's little more than nostalgia for a biblical past that never existed. I can prove that by his own statistics. He identifies sites with only 5 to 20 percent of the earliest cooking pots as having been established only in the mid- to late-12th century or even the 11th century B.C.E. But the point is that if there are *any* early cooking pots there at all, then the site was established in the early 12th century. It may have been small, it may have grown later; but it has to have been established in the earliest phase of settlement. In short, there *was* no general movement of peoples from east to west. You have to bear in mind that Zertal is relying only on a surface survey. A surface survey means that archaeologists pick up the few fragments of pottery that they find on the surface of the ground. On a small site like Zertal's, you might pick up sherds from ten or fifteen cooking pots. Statistics based on that kind of sample are worse than meaningless. You can't really prove much of anything on the basis of surface surveys alone. But even Zertal's crude statistics prove him wrong.

Another survey was conducted by Israel Finkelstein in the tribal territory of Ephraim. He reported it in his 1988 work which is now the standard treatment, *The Archaeology of the Israelite Settlement,* a very fine book that is already revolutionizing biblical scholarship.[9] That doesn't mean, however, that Finkelstein is correct in every detail. He reports on 115 sites in his survey area. He, too, argues that the earliest sites are in the east; but instead of deriving the settlers from across the Jordan, he believes they came from western Palestine itself. However, Finkelstein does not say that they came from the Canaanite urban centers. He believes that they were local pastoral nomads who had been there for centuries, but now are simply moving up into the hill country. But I want to point out one thing. Far to the west, on the western slopes of the hill country is Finkelstein's own site of 'Izbet Sartah, and by his own admission it was established at the end of the 13th century B.C.E. It is one of the *earliest* of all the proto-Israelite sites. How then can the settlers be moving from east to west? It looks rather like they are moving from west to east.

Furthermore, even if you could show that the sites on the eastern side of the central ridge were the earliest, that too could be explained. If you were a refugee fleeing from the Canaanite city-states along the coast, where would you go? To the other side of the ridge, where it's safer. And what would you do 15 years later, when conditions had settled down a bit? You would migrate back to the west where there is better pastureland and better agricultural land.

So the above theories, based upon ceramic typology and relative statistics derived from surface surveys, can be very misleading. In the back of the minds of both these Israeli scholars—Finkelstein and Zertal—I believe there lingers a fondness for Albrecht Alt's old explanation of Israelite origins in terms of peaceful infiltration, in this case from Transjordan. But I must stress that the Israeli archaeologists have not been able to handle the material from Jordan—for obvious reasons. There is very little archaeological material from anywhere in Jordan that would provide a background of pastoral nomadism out of which the early Israelites could have come.

Now let us review a few features quickly. The typical proto-Israelite site contains clusters of houses featuring a central courtyard, with sleeping and living areas for the family on the second floor. The flat roof would be useful for drying food stuffs and preparing food. If you visit an Arab village in the West Bank today, you can still see such houses in use. I've seen them all across Greece and Italy, around Syria and Turkey, down into Jordan. The point is that these ancient houses are not necessarily "Israelite" houses in themselves. They are simply very practical farmhouses of the type that begins to proliferate in the early Iron I period. The early Israelites borrowed this house plan, as they borrowed a great many other things.

What emerges from our survey of proto-Israelite sites is a kind of *composite* culture, in which there are both old and new features. The use of courtyard houses is new. The kind of social and economic structure that they reflect is also new. But the technology—in pottery and in metalworking—reflects a great deal of continuity with the previous societies of the Canaanite Late Bronze Age. The early Israelites are best seen as homesteaders—pioneer farmers settling the hill-country frontier of central Palestine, which had

been sparsely occupied before Iron I. They were not pastoral nomads who had originally migrated all the way from Mesopotamia, as
the biblical tradition describes them, moving along the edges of the
Fertile Crescent up into Syria and then penetrating down into Palestine. Nor were the early Israelites like the modern Bedouin who
still inhabit the area. They may not have been primarily sheepherders, although some may have been stockbreeders. For the most
part, the early Israelites were agriculturalists from the fringes of
Canaanite society.

It is true that the stories in Genesis seem to reflect a pastoral
nomadic background. But here we are dealing with *literature*, not
with history. There is no reason to believe that the majority of the
ancestors of the Israelites had been pastoral nomads, much less barbarians sweeping in from the desert. They were displaced Canaanites.
For the most part, they came from various elements of Canaanite
society who decided to settle the hill-country frontier.

In a recent issue of *Biblical Archaeology Review* there is the
relief of Ramesses II that Hershel spoke about, which some scholars
believe was recarved by Merneptah.* One scene depicts the siege of
Ashkelon, now being excavated by Larry Stager. Above the Egyptian
inscription identifying Ashkelon there is a group of people that Frank
Yurco thinks are Israelites. Merneptah, in his famous "Victory Stele,"
claims to have destroyed a people called Israelites, so he must have
been familiar with what they looked like. Yurco believes this scene is
an actual eyewitness portrait of early Israelites. On the other hand,
Anson Rainey, an Israeli scholar, believes that somewhere else on
the relief is another group of people who are Israelites.** I suggest,
however, that we do not have any reliable eyewitness portraits of
what early Israelites looked like. And from the point of view of the
archaeological remains, we know very little about their ideology
or their religious beliefs and practices. But we know a lot about
their social and economic structure. We know a lot about their
technology. We know a lot about the demography of the regions
they were settling.

* See Frank J. Yurco, "3,200-Year-Old Picture of Israelites Found in Egypt," *Biblical Archaeol-
ogy Review*, September/October 1990.
** See "Anson F. Rainey's Challenge" and "Yurco's Response," both in *Biblical Archaeology
Review*, November/December 1991.

Let us return now to our original questions: Who were the Israelites? Where did they come from? And how were they different from the Canaanites?

In my judgment, on the basis of both the archaeological evidence and an understanding of the biblical text, particularly the tradition preserved in the Book of Judges, the early Israelites were a motley lot—urban refugees, people from the countryside, what we might call "social bandits," brigands of various kinds, malcontents, dropouts from society. They may have been social revolutionaries, as some scholars hold, imbued with Yahwistic fervor, although that's not traceable archaeologically. They may have had some notion of religious reforms of one sort or another. There does appear to be a kind of primitive democracy reflected in the settlements and the remains of their material culture.

Perhaps this group of people included some pastoral nomads, even some from Transjordan. I'm even willing to grant that a small nucleus of people who became Israelites had originally been in Egypt, as Baruch Halpern suggests in his analysis of the literary tradition. (This is the only way that you can save the literary tradition; otherwise you will have to jettison it completely.) Thus, it is quite possible that there were some newcomers in this mixture of peoples, who were, however, mostly indigenous Canaanites. And all of them were indeed newcomers to the hill country. They were settling down *there* for the first time; that is what is new. What is old, however, is their technology, particularly their pottery, their language and their script, factors that indicate a rather strong cultural continuity, despite a new ethnic consciousness.

In short, if you had been walking in the countryside of central Palestine, especially in the hill country, in the 12th or 11th century B.C.E. and had met several people, you could probably not have distinguished Israelites from Canaanites or Canaanites from Philistines. They probably looked alike and dressed alike and spoke alike. But the kinds of things that now enable us to talk about ethnicity will have disappeared from the archaeological record.

So how do we know the people in question *were* Israelites? My solution is a rather simple one. First of all, we have not only the biblical tradition that calls them Israelites, but we also have the Merneptah Stele that proves beyond any shadow of a doubt that there was a distinct ethnic group in Palestine before 1200, one that not only called itself "Israelite" but was known to the Egyptians as "Israelite." That need not be the same as later biblical Israel; but the label "Israelite," which I want to apply to these early Iron I sites, is not one that I invented. It's attested in the literary tradition, both biblical and non-biblical.

Another point is this: In the tenth century B.C.E. and later, at the time of the Israelite monarchy—and no one doubts the existence of that—you have the continuation of the material culture at which we have been looking. All you have to do is push that assemblage, as archaeologists call it, back into the 11th and 12th century. If it was Israelite in the 10th century B.C.E., then it was Israelite in the 12th century B.C.E. For these reasons, I use the term "Israelite" for the early Iron I hill-country settlements, although I use it in quotes, and I prefer to speak of "proto-Israelite" settlements.

The model I've advanced here is useful, probably the best model we have at the moment. But remember what a model is: a hypothesis, meant to be proven or disproven. Perhaps we will see it all differently in another ten or fifteen years.

Suppose that we were to excavate a site we presumed to be Israelite, identified by a modern Arabic name that was the same as the biblical name. Suppose that we found a destruction layer, a nice big, healthy destruction layer—thick ashes, smashed pottery, everybody killed, just what archaeologists like. And suppose that above that stratum we found a new style of pottery, new burial customs and a new material culture. And suppose that we get really lucky and find a monumental stele that says "I, Joshua ben-Nun, on this Tuesday morning, April (laughter) the 9th, in the year 1207 B.C.E., destroyed this site in the name of Yahweh, the God of Israel." You might say that such a discovery would be archaeological *proof* of the historicity of the biblical tradition. That's exactly what an earlier generation thought. But it is not. After all, what is the claim of the Hebrew Bible? Not that Israel took Canaan, but that Yahweh gave Canaan to the people of Israel. That's a theological assertion, which cannot be proven by archaeology—and it can't be disproven, either. The point is that centuries later, as the writers and editors of the Hebrew Bible looked back upon their own experience, they could not understand how they had gotten where they were. They could not explain their own origins. To them it seemed a miracle. And who are we, their spiritual heirs, to disagree?[10]

ENDNOTES

1. For recent syntheses of the following discussion, see Israel Finkelstein, *The Archaeology of the Israelite Settlement* (Jerusalem: Israel Exploration Society, 1988); William G. Dever, *Recent Archaeological Discoveries and Biblical Research* (Seattle: Univ. of Washington Press, 1990), chapter 2, and "Tell el-Dab'a and Levantine Middle Bronze Age Chronology: A Rejoinder," *Bulletin of the American Schools of Oriental Research* (*BASOR*) 281 (1991), pp. 73-77.

2. On Mt. Ebal, see Adam Zertal, "An Early Iron Age Cultic Site on Mt. Ebal: Excavation Seasons 1982-1987," *Tel Aviv* 13-14 (1986-1987), pp. 105-165, and "Has Joshua's Altar Been Found on Mt. Ebal?" *Biblical Archaeology Review* (*BAR*), Jan./Feb. 1985, pp. 26-43; but cf. Aharon Kempinski, "Joshua's Altar—An Iron Age I Watchtower," *BAR*, Jan./Feb. 1986, pp. 42-49. See also Zertal, "How Could Kempinski Be So Wrong?" *BAR*, Jan./Feb. 1986, pp. 43, 49-53; Anson F. Rainey, "Zertal's Altar—A Blatant Phony," *BAR*, July/Aug. 1986, p. 66.

3. On the bull site, see Amihai Mazar, "The 'Bull Site'—An Iron I Open Cult Place," *BASOR* 247 (1982), pp. 27-41; "Bronze Bull Found in Israelite 'High Place' from the Time of the Judges," *BAR*, Sept./Oct. 1983, pp. 34-40; Hershel Shanks, "Two Early Israelite Cult Sites Now Questioned," *BAR*, Jan./Feb. 1988, pp. 48-52.

4. On Khirbet Raddana, see Lawrence E. Stager, "The Archaeology of the Family in Ancient Israel," *BASOR* 260 (1985), pp. 1-36.

5. Stager, "Archaeology of the Family" and "The Song of Deborah—Why Some Tribes Answered the Call and Others Did Not," *BAR*, Jan./Feb. 1989, pp. 50-64.

6. For details, see Dever, "Ceramic Continuity, Ethnicity in the Archaeological Record, and the Question of Israelite Origins," *Eretz-Israel* (Malamat volume), forthcoming.

7. On 'Izbet Sartah, see Finkelstein, in *Archaeology of the Israelite Settlement*; *'Izbet Sartah. An Early Iron Age Site Near Rosh Ha'ayin, Israel*, British Archaeological Records International Series (Oxford, 1986); see also the review by Dever, *BASOR* 284 (1991), pp. 77-90. Aaron Demsky and Moshe Kochavi, "An Israelite Village from the Days of the Judges," pp. 19-21, and "An Alphabet from the Days of the Judges," pp. 23-30, both in *BAR*, Sept./Oct. 1978.

8. On Tel Masos, see Dever, "Archaeology and Israelite Origins: A Review Article," *BASOR* 279 (1990), pp. 89-95. See also Volkmar Fritz, "Conquest or Settlement? The Early Iron Age in Palestine," *Biblical Archaeologist* 50 (1987), pp. 84-100; Aharon Kempinski, "Israelite Conquest or Settlement? New Light from Tel Masos," *BAR*, Sept. 1976, pp. 25-30.

9. See sources cited in endnotes 1 and 7.

10. For further reading, see references in previously cited articles to a rapidly expanding literature. See, for example, Fritz, "Conquest or Settlement?"; Dever, "Unresolved Issues in the Early History of Israel: Toward a Synthesis of Archaeological Reconstructions," in *The Politics of Exegesis: Essays in Honor of Norman K. Gottwald* (Boston: Pilgrim, 1992).

Questions & Answers

Sir, as I understand it, pottery found in Avaris in Egypt is a Canaanite type. If that's so, isn't it possible that the people did come from the Goshen area and had a tradition of Canaanite-style pottery.

Yes, Hershel mentioned that earlier. But the point is that the Canaanite pottery in question is the pottery of the last phase of the Middle Bronze Age—from about 1650 to about 1550 B.C.E.—centuries before the emergence of Israel. It can have no possible connection. I have argued vociferously with Manfred Bietak, the excavator of the site, showing that his material is indeed Canaanite, which means—exactly as Hershel said—that large numbers of Asiatics were penetrating into the eastern Delta in the first half of the second millennium B.C.E. Baruch [Halpern] touches on that too. That may indeed provide a historical nucleus out of which the later biblical stories came.

I would like to be the first to say that I give full assent to everything Baruch says. It is highly likely, I think, that among the principal editors of the biblical tradition were people who belonged to the so-called house of Joseph, parts of the tribes of Benjamin, Judah and Manasseh. And, indeed, among them there probably were people who had been in Egypt who, in one way or another, thought that they had miraculously escaped. What they have done, however, is to impose their own experience upon many other peoples who came rather from Canaan. Israel was a confederation of peoples. The Bible hints of that already. Remember that passage in Ezekiel: "You are of the land of Canaan; your father was an Amorite and your mother a Hittite" (Ezekiel 16:3). The Israelites remembered their own ancestry. What they did later, in the literary tradition, was to neaten it up a bit, to make it all-inclusive, "all Israel." The cultural unity implied in the biblical narrative was probably not present in actual fact in the 13th and 12th centuries B.C.E., but only developed later. I think that the unifying factor probably *was* Yahwism, but that we can't trace archaeologically. So, yes, there are roots. As for the Late Bronze Age Canaanite storage jars found in Egypt, which

Hershel mentioned, these are trade items; they are shown being off-loaded from Canaanite ships by Egyptians. This has nothing to do with ethnic movements. All this is to say that yes, some of the ancestors of Israel may have been in Egypt, but it's quite clear now that by no means all of them were.

You spoke of the majority of the Israelites coming from a Canaanite background and moving up into the hill country, a rather difficult terrain on which to subsist. Where did they come from literally, and why did they go there?

I don't think we can be too precise about that. I have suggested they came both from the urban Canaanite centers of the Late Bronze Age as well as from the countryside. I don't believe you can build agricultural terraces overnight; I don't believe you can learn to breed cattle overnight. I think these newcomers were experienced farmers for the most part, although not necessarily Norman Gottwald's "peasant farmers." The term "peasant" is from later periods and should not be applied to early Israel. These folk were experienced farmers and stockbreeders, probably not peasants but freeholders. They were not foreigners at all; they were displaced Canaanites. We can't locate them more precisely than that.

Well, if they were urban Canaanites, where did they get their farming experience?

As I've said, I don't think all of them were, or even most of them. Among them there were possibly refugees from the urban centers who might already have been in the countryside for a generation or more. From the Amarna letters, we know that the Canaanite city-states were collapsing as early as 1400 B.C.E. There was a mass exodus from these Canaanite cities, so there was already present a large rural population, which was always in flux. The hill country provided the perfect retreat for them. It is precisely what modern Christian and other dissident groups have done in southern Lebanon today; they have retreated to the hill country. The situation is very similar.

As a collateral question to what has just been asked, are you saying that the major social, economic and political unit remained the *mishpachah*, the family?

Yes. Archaeologically we are able to comment on social history; that's what seems most amenable to us. As an archaeologist, I would describe early Israel as an agrarian social movement, probably with a strong reformist base, as such movements have often had in history. Beyond that, I don't think the archaeologist can go. But it is the *agrarian* character that fits perfectly with both Joshua and Judges, as well as Samuel 1 and 2.

Would some of them—since they came from disparate backgrounds, technologically speaking—would some of them perhaps have been experts in metalworking?

Some of them, perhaps, knew iron working well, just as they knew primitive pottery making. But it is all local. In other words, the basic socioeconomic structure is the family, producing its own economic necessities. I think that later Israelite society and religion grew out of that. And that is absolutely in the spirit of the biblical traditions.

You described two villages close by each other. One was clearly a Canaanite site in which there was a certain kind of pottery, and then nearby was an Israelite site. How do we know that the pottery of the type you were speaking of in the latter was not a trade item?

Because it's all the pottery there is at the site; you'd have to argue that all the pottery was traded into the site, not just a few items. The total ceramic repertoire at both sites is indeed similar, but the difference is this. At Ebenezer ('Izbet Sartah, if it is indeed Israelite Ebenezer), you have a completely different house-form from Canaanite Aphek, you have a completely different economy and social structure. At Aphek you have the large palace of a ruler, with cuneiform documents, reflecting a literate urban society. Ebenezer is a small farming village a few miles away. And although the pottery is the same, I think that the people are very different—in other words, a different *ethnic* group. I didn't define "ethnicity," but you all know what it is. When a people, a social group, begin to think of themselves as being different, they are. And that's exactly what early Israel was—an ethnic group, which, already in the 12th century, had a self-conscious identity, a sense of "peoplehood." The picture of that identity changed and grew in the Hebrew Bible, but already in the 12th century B.C.E, Israelites knew that they were different. That doesn't mean, however, that the early Israelites were unique; they were different, and they knew themselves to be different.

To conclude, you don't just look at a single pot; you look at the whole pottery repertoire. And you don't look only at the pottery; you look at the whole site. You have to compare things in that way.

What made them different?

As I say, according to the biblical tradition, it was not only their religious faith but their moral superiority. I can't comment on that as an archaeologist. I do suspect that religion was a powerful factor in social change, as it often has been. But here we are dependent on our textual scholars. Happily, the last talk today is to be presented by Kyle McCarter, who's given a lot of thought to that. He will talk about Yahwism and how it emerged. I'm simply trying to be honest about the limitations of the archaeological evidence. We can't really deal with political or religious history very well. We can, however, deal with social and economic history. And we can take a label from the text and affix it to a material culture and say this looks to us as though it may be "Israelite." But final proof is always lacking—which is what keeps us in business and allows me to travel to visit with you. (Laughter.) Thank you.

INTRODUCTION

*B*ecause *Professor Dever directly commented on the views of three other major scholars—Israel Finkelstein, Norman Gottwald and Adam Zertal—who have played a significant part in the debates on the emergence of Israel, we have given them an opportunity to respond to Professor Dever in this printed version of the symposium. Following their remarks is Professor Dever's reply to these additional responses.*

Responses

ISRAEL FINKELSTEIN
Institute of Archaeology, Tel Aviv University

B efore engaging in yet another duel with Bill Dever, this time on his recent theory on the origin of the "proto-Israelites," I wish to say I share Hershel Shanks' esteem for his scholarship. There is no doubt that Dever is one of the leading biblical archaeologists on the scene today; my debates with him—on the fortifications of Gezer, on the nature of the Intermediate Bronze Age and now on the rise of early Israel—have always been accompanied by a deep appreciation for his field work and for his theoretical contributions to the field of Palestinian archaeology.

In his talk, Dever adopts a Gottwaldian approach to the emergence of early Israel. His theory rests on three pillars, all suggested as early as the 1970s by supporters of Gottwald's social-revolution hypothesis. These three "pillars" of conventional wisdom were all discredited in the 1980s in light of new data that have been revealed in comprehensive field work—surveys and excavations—in the central hill country of Israel. This brief response to Dever's discussion begins with an examination of the three pillars supporting his theory.

(Shaky) Pillar One: The emergence of Israel in the highlands of Canaan was made possible by two technological innovations. Dever adheres to Albright's half-century old theory,[1] that the Iron I wave of settlement in the highlands was a result of a new skill—that of hewing water cisterns: "In fact, one of the reasons that the area was never effectively settled before the Iron Age was that the art of digging cisterns had not yet been perfected." There are three grave flaws in this hypothesis:

A. The central hill country of Canaan was already quite densely settled in the Early Bronze Age and again in the Middle Bronze Age.[2]

B. The results of the 1968 survey have proven beyond any doubt that the knowledge of hewing water cisterns had already been mastered in the Middle Bronze Age,[3] and most probably even earlier, in the Early Bronze Age. Scores of Early and Middle Bronze sites are located in hilly areas devoid of any permanent water sources.[4] The hewing of plastered water cisterns was therefore an outcome of the penetration into these "dry" areas, rather than the factor that opened the way to the expansion into these geographical niches.

C. Many of the Iron I highlands sites are devoid of such water cisterns; apparently, their inhabitants brought water from distant springs and stored it in the typical large Iron I *pithoi.*[5]

Dever adds that terracing, too, "was a new technology, perfected in the late 13th and early 12th centuries B.C.E.," and that it enabled the proto-Israelites (Dever's excellent name for the early Iron I settlers in the highlands of Canaan) to exploit the highlands frontier. He further argues that the sophisticated skill of building terraces indicates that their builders came from a rural, sedentary background. This theory was also proposed long ago, when the knowledge of the settlement history of the highlands was still in its infancy.[6] It is now clear that the Iron I settlement process began in areas of the hill country that did not require the construction of terraces—the desert fringe, the intermontane valleys of the central range, and flat areas, such as the Bethel plateau. Moreover, the Middle Bronze activity on the western slopes of the highlands—where cultivation without terracing is almost impossible—seems to indicate that terrace construction was already carried out at that time. There is good reason to believe that terracing was practiced even before, in the Early Bronze Age, with the first widespread cultivation of olives

and grapevines in the hill country.[7] Terracing was therefore an outcome of the demographic expansion into the rugged parts of the hill
country and the beginning of highlands horticulture, rather than an
innovation that made this expansion possible. The terraces indicate
that their builders practiced horticulture; they tell us nothing about
the origin of these people.

*(Shaky) Pillar Two: There is a clear continuity in the material
culture between the Late Bronze Age sites of the lowlands and the
Iron I sites of the highlands; this proves, according to Dever, that the
inhabitants of the latter originated from the sedentary population of
the former.* According to Dever, "the common early Israelite pottery
turns out to be nearly identical to that of the late 13th century
B.C.E.; it comes right out of the Late Bronze Age urban Canaanite
repertoire."[8] Indeed, certain Iron I highlands types of pottery do
resemble Late Bronze vessels. But at the same time, there are some
fundamental differences; the Iron I highlands assemblages are poor
and limited compared to the rich, decorated and varied assemblages
of the Late Bronze Age.

In any case, the essential question is whether we can learn
about the origin of the makers/users from the ceramic repertoire.
Ceramic traditions are influenced by the environment of settlements,
by the socioeconomic conditions of the makers/users, by earlier traditions, by conventions of nearby regions and, in certain cases of
migration, by customs brought by the settlers from their original
homeland. In the case of the highlands of Canaan in Iron I, signs of
continuity of Late Bronze traditions show no more than certain
influence from Iron I lowlands sites, which still practiced at that
time the pottery traditions of the previous period; signs of discontinuity reflect the fact that the highlands people lived in small isolated,
rural, almost autarchic, communities. Both the continuity and the
discontinuity indicate environmental and socioeconomic conditions
rather than direct roots in the Late Bronze lowlands.

The same holds true for the architectural traditions of the early
Iron Age highlands sites, especially the four-room house. Dever's
claim that the early Israelites "borrowed this house plan, as they
borrowed a great many other things" is disproved by the fact that
intensive research of over a century, in dozens of Late Bronze sites,

has failed to reveal even one Late Bronze prototype of this house plan.[9] The four-room houses were gradually developed in Iron I in order to adapt to the hilly environment of the settlers.

The material culture of the Iron I highlands sites cannot provide the desired answer to the riddle of the origin of the proto-Israelites. We should turn therefore to the other branch of modern archaeology—the study of the dispersal of human communities over the landscape, that is, settlement patterns.

(Shaky) Pillar Three: The wave of settlement in Iron I was the first significant settlement process in the history of the hill country. Dever states that the central hill country of Palestine "had been sparsely occupied before Iron I," a statement which leads him to the conclusion that the Iron I people came from the lowlands. This assertion, too, fits the status of archaeological research in the 1960s. Recent surveys have shown that the region was intensively occupied twice before Iron I—in the Early Bronze Age, when dozens of sites were established in the area between the Jezreel and the Beer-Sheva valleys, and in the Middle Bronze Age, when about 250 sites were founded in this region.[10] These data are crucial for understanding the settlement process under discussion here.

As for the later history of the proto-Israelite sites, Dever claims that most of them "were abandoned in the tenth century B.C.E." That may be true for some of the excavated Iron I sites such as 'Izbet Sartah, Giloh, Khirbet Raddana and Ai—in fact, most of these sites were chosen for excavation for that very reason: the Iron I remains were easy to uncover—but the majority of Iron I sites in the hill country continued to be occupied throughout the Iron Age. In southern Samaria, for instance, only 22 of the 115 Iron I sites (19 percent) were deserted in Iron II, 76 of the sites even expanded in Iron II.

Dever also takes issue with the results of my excavations at 'Izbet Sartah, a site located in the foothills of Samaria, overlooking the coastal plain near Aphek. Dever does not accept my reconstruction of the layout of stratum III at this key site as an oval settlement with a large central courtyard surrounded by a row of broadrooms, on the ground that the remains are too scanty. He further argues that the 'Izbet Sartah finds indicate that the Iron I highlands people came from lowlands urban or rural background. A close look at the plan of the site reveals that almost 40 percent of the total length of its peripheral wall was uncovered, together with the remains of seven of the adjacent broadrooms. That is enough for a reasonable reconstruction. The reconstruction of stratum III is based on a comparison with other Iron Age sites in different parts of the country, a method that Dever embraced in his recent illuminating review of my 'Izbet Sartah report and my *Archaeology of the Israelite Settlement*.[11]

Dever then opposes my theory on the origin of the people of 'Izbet Sartah: "How then can the settlers be moving from east to west? It looks rather like they are moving from west to east." In all my work on early Israel, I emphasized that in the early stages of Iron I the settlers opted for ecological niches that were convenient for a subsistence economy based on dry farming and animal husbandry. Data on the economy of premodern Arab villages in the vicinity of 'Izbet Sartah indicate exactly this kind of subsistence. Unlike Adam Zertal, I have never tried to portray a direct east-west movement of the proto-Israelites; rather, I described it as a gradual shift from regions adapted for a grain-growing–herding economy (desert fringe, eastern flank of the central range of the central hill country, foothills, etc.) to niches convenient mainly for horticulture (the western slopes of the central range). This geographical and economic expansion also sheds light on the political development of the early Israelites.[12]

We are able to trace these demographic developments by a meticulous study of the pottery collected in dozens of survey sites. But surprisingly, Dever dismisses the importance of quantitative analysis of survey assemblages, claiming that in a small Iron I site in the highlands "you might pick up sherds from ten or fifteen cooking pots. Statistics based on that kind of sample are worse than meaningless." However, in the study of survey pottery, it is not the single site with 10 or 15 sherds that is important, but the overall picture of a region. Thus, a quantitative analysis based on over 100 sites, each yielding 10 or 15 sherds, is no less reliable than most statistics provided by careful excavations.

To sum up, old-fashioned, cisterns-terraces-pots solutions to the problem of the emergence of early Israel leave us in the same miserable spot where we stood two decades ago. They should be replaced by the following observations, which are based on new data revealed in the comprehensive surveys conducted in the hill country in recent years:

1. The emergence of Israel in Canaan must be viewed with a long perspective.[13] Investigation of any complex settlement process should start several centuries before it commenced and end after it ripened. Applying this rule to the problem of the origin of the Israelites, one must start with the settlement developments in the Middle Bronze Age and end with the demographic processes of Iron II.

2. The settlement process in the highlands in Iron I was a third peak in a cyclic history of alternative demographic expansion and decay. These developments included three waves of settlement (in the Early Bronze I, Middle Bronze IIB-C and Iron I), with two periods of severe settlement crisis between them (Intermediate Bronze Age and Late Bronze Age).[14] The settlement of the proto-Israelites was therefore one phase in a two-millennia-long process that came to an end with the rise of the national territorial states of Iron II. Any attempt to understand the emergence of early Israel without taking into consideration this background is doomed to failure.

3. The geographical dichotomy between highlands and lowlands in the southern Levant, as well as in other parts of the ancient Near East and the Mediterranean world, led to the formation of different social, economic and political structures. Therefore, some of the characteristics of the Iron I hill country of Canaan can be more usefully compared to distant hilly regions, rather than to the nearby lowlands.[15]

4. In the highlands of Canaan, as in other frontier regions in the southern Levant, there was always a significant pastoral element in the population. The share of the pastoral groups grew in times of settlement crisis and shrank in periods of stability and prosperity.[16] The emergence of Israel was part of these demographic oscillations: The breakdown of the political system of the Middle Bronze Age led to the nomadization of a significant part of the population of the highlands frontier; in the Late Bronze Age these pastoral groups lived in a close symbiotic relationship with the remaining urban centers. Another crisis in the urban system occurred at the end of the Late Bronze and demolished these symbiotic relations, forcing the pastoralists to settle down. Other groups—local and foreign, pastoral and sedentary—also settled in the hill country in the course of the upheaval in the Late Bronze–Iron I transition, including cer-

tain elements from the collapsing sedentary system in the lowlands. These diverse groups crystallized in a slow and gradual process into the early Israelite monarchy of the tenth century B.C.E.

Dever does not take into consideration these observations. Instead, he follows the biblical tradition, seeing the emergence of Israel as a unique phenomenon—an "event," rather than a phase, in a long, cyclic historical process.

ENDNOTES

1. William F. Albright, *The Archaeology of Palestine* (Harmondsworth, UK: 1949), p. 113.

2. Israel Finkelstein and Ram Gophna, "Settlement, Demographic and Economic Patterns in the Highlands of Palestine in the Chalcolithic and Early Bronze Periods and the Beginning of Urbanism," forthcoming in *Bulletin of the American Schools of Oriental Research (BASOR)*; Finkelstein, "The Central Hill Country in the Intermediate Bronze Age," *Israel Exploration Journal* 41 (1991), pp. 27-30.

3. Ram Gophna and Yosef Porath, "The Land of Ephraim and Manasseh," in *Judaea, Samaria and the Golan*, ed. M. Kochavi (Jerusalem: Archaeological Survey of Israel, 1972), p. 197 (in Hebrew).

4. Israel Finkelstein, "The Land of Ephraim Survey 1980-1987: Preliminary Report," *Tel Aviv* 15-16 (1988-1989), pp. 136-144.

5. Adam Zertal, "The Water Factor during the Israelite Settlement Process in Canaan," in *Society and Economy in the Eastern Mediterranean* (c. 1500-1000 B.C.), ed. M. Heltzer and E. Lipinski (Louvain: Uitgeverij Peeters, 1988), pp. 341-352.

6. For instance, C.H.J. de Geus, "The Importance of Archaeological Research into the Palestinian Agricultural Terrraces, with an Excursus of the Hebrew Word *gbi*," *Palestine Exploration Quarterly* 107 (1975), pp. 65-74; G.W. Ahlstrom, "Where Did the Israelites Live?" *Journal of Near Eastern Studies* 41 (1982), pp. 133-138.

7. Shimon Gibson, B. Ibbs and Amos Kloner, "The Sataf Project of Landscape Archaeology in the Judaean Hills: A Preliminary Report on Four Seasons of Survey and Excavations (1987-1989)," *Levant* 23 (1991), p. 48.

8. See already H.J. Franken, "Palestine in the Time of the Nineteenth Dynasty, (b) Archaeological Evidence," *Cambridge Ancient History* II/2, ed. I.E. Edwards (Cambridge, UK: Cambridge Univ. Press, 1981), p. 337; J. Maxwell Miller, "The Israelite Occupation of Canaan," in *Israelite and Judean History*, ed. J.H. Hayes and Miller (London: SCM, 1977), pp. 255, 262.

9. As far as I can judge, not even the pillared building found at Tel Batash—George L. Kelm and Amihai Mazar, "Three Seasons of Excavations at Tel Batash—Biblical Timnah," *BASOR* 248 (1982), pp. 9-12.

10. See endnote 2.

11. William G. Dever, "Archaeological Data on the Israelite Settlement: A Review of Two Recent Works," *BASOR* 284 (1991), pp. 77-90.

12. Israel Finkelstein, "The Emergence of the Monarchy in Israel: The Environmental and Socio-Economic Aspects," *Journal for the Study of the Old Testament* 44 (1989), pp. 43-74.

13. See already Albrecht Alt, "Die Landnahme der Israeliten in Palastina," *Reformationsprogramm der Universitat Leipzig* (Leipzig, 1925); English transl., *Essays in Old Testament History and Religion* (Oxford: Blackwell, 1966), pp. 135-169.

14. Israel Finkelstein, "The Emergence of Israel: A Phase in the Cyclic History of Canaan in the Third and Second Millennia BCE," in *From Nomadism to Monarchy: Archaeological and Historical Aspects of Early Israel*, ed. N. Naaman and Finkelstein, forthcoming.

15. See, for instance, Leon Marfoe, "The Integrative Transformation: Patterns of Socio-Political Organization in Southern Syria," *BASOR* 234 (1979), pp. 1-42.

16. For similar settlement oscillations in Transjordan in recent centuries, see Norman N. Lewis, *Nomads and Settlers in Syria and Jordan, 1800-1980* (Cambridge, UK: Cambridge Univ. Press, 1987).

NORMAN K. GOTTWALD
New York Theological Seminary

As usual, I am impressed by William Dever's balanced and temperate reading of the archaeological data and I agree with virtually all of his generalizing characterizations of early Israel, particularly his judgment that it was an agrarian social movement lacking specialized elites. I am also in accord with his call for a more attentive and nuanced study of its social and economic history. Like Lawrence Stager's article on the Israelite family, which he cites with praise, Dever's own discussion is rich in contributions toward just such a social and economic history.

By contrast, Dever is theoretically "adrift at sea" when he tries to attach a working model of society to the archaeological data he has assessed. Unfortunately, Dever fails to see that an agrarian social revolutionary reading of Israel's communitarian society makes far more comprehensive sense of his detailed description of early Israel than does the "symbiosis" construct he puts forth.

In my view, symbiosis is not really a comprehensive model at all; instead, it is a valuable but restricted hypothesis asserting that Israel slowly gained ground in the highlands without breaking decisively with all, or even most, aspects of Canaanite culture. Symbiosis tells us something about Israel's point of departure, chiefly that Israel was not a *de novo* creation, but it does not tell us much about the socioeconomic lineaments of emerging Israel, particularly the junctures at which Israel began to distinguish itself from the rest of Canaan. Symbiosis is therefore one of the preconditions for, even one of the first steps in, developing a far more comprehensive and multidimensional model of Israel as a social transformation within Canaan, achieved by Canaanites on the way to becoming an autonomous society and culture.

A major reason for Dever's lapse at the point of developing a covering theory is that he seems uninformed about recent developments in social-critical theory concerning early Israel. For example, he apparently does not realize that since 1985 I have abandoned the terms "peasant revolt" and "egalitarian society" as imprecise and misleading explanatory categories for early Israel, or that I have replaced them with constructs of "agrarian social revolution" and "communitarian mode of production." The result is that Dever's comments on my modeling of early Israel have as much currency as would an attempt on my part to assess Dever's archaeological interpretations based exclusively on his work prior to 1985. Also, although I realize that the format of the symposium does not call for documentation, I see no sign that Dever recognizes the pertinence of the work of many other contributors to early Israelite social history, among whom I would name Robert B. Coote and Keith Whitelam,[1] James W. Flanagan,[2] Neils P. Lemche[3] and William H. Stiebing, Jr.,[4] for starters.

Dever thus leaves us with two feeble alternatives: either an outmoded, pre-1985 peasant revolt theory that all social theorists of early Israel have advanced beyond, or a symbiosis theory that explains only a small part of what needs to be explained.

What do I mean by conceiving of early Israel as a communitarian social revolution? I mean that Israelites became free agrarians who enjoyed the full use of their own surpluses, unlike other Canaanite cultivators who were constantly endangered by taxation and debt payments. "Public services" promised and erratically delivered by city-states, such as defense and administration of justice, were provided in Israel by intertribal networking. Meanwhile, the cult of Yahweh, with its attendant religious ideology, expressed the interests and values of the communitarian movement.

This major shift in the mode of production prevailed over a considerable territory in the Canaanite highlands for some two centuries.

But does this historically modest achievement really deserve to be called a social revolution? My considered judgment is that it does. But it is critical to acknowledge that how one reasons for or against that conclusion is closely connected with the disputed issue of "social intentionality" in early Israel. What were these people up to? How did the Israelite communitarian mode of production happen to emerge? Was it preplanned? Was it consciously shaped in midcourse? Was it an inhibiting cultural legacy? Was it an unwanted historical accident?

As I see it, three basic viewpoints have been suggested on this issue. Some believe that Israel's communitarian mode of production was a carryover from its earlier lifestyle of pastoral nomadism, and was thus a wholly predictable cultural inheritance which Israel outgrew as it settled down. Others believe that communitarianism developed in Canaan because of a breakdown of the city-states so massive that rural communities were thrown on their own resources and learned to cooperate to survive, and thus reluctantly adopted a lesser-of-evils strategy for coping with an undesired happenstance. Still others, myself among them, believe that this communitarianism—however much aided by city-state decline—was an insurgent movement recruited among a coalition of peasants, pastoralists, mercenaries, bandits and disaffected state and temple functionaries who simultaneously worked to oppose city-state control over them and to develop a countersociety, and the result was therefore, in substantial measure, "intended" by them. This is not to say that Israelites were in agreement on all aspects of social organization, or that they all adhered to the agreements and institutions they worked out, or that they were able to foresee the consequences of what they were doing. It does mean that by and large they wanted to be free of state sovereignty and, in its place, to develop loosely coordinated self-rule, despite all the problems that decentralization created for them.

Dever and I are in agreement that Israel's communitarianism was not the legacy of pastoral nomadism, but I do not see that Dever's inclination toward symbiosis yields us anything more than a formal restatement of what is evident about the cultural and technological overlap between Canaan and Israel.

I think the immediate challenge for Dever and the archaeologists is this: If we grant that early Israel displayed a communitarian self-sufficiency that increasingly distinguished it from other Canaanite peoples, does a social reading of the archaeological record reveal signs of communal purposefulness on the part of the Israelite highlanders? Dever repeats what I, too, have often said: We don't see any evidence of a social revolution in the archaeological data. But are we correct in this judgment? What have we been looking for? What do we think would count as such evidence? Inscriptions? More destroyed cities in the highlands? Have we been looking for overt political and military evidence to the neglect of the more subtle cumulative social evidence?

If we take the societal data we have in hand, Dever points the way when he refers to Lawrence Stager's social interpretation of the early Israelite housing complexes. Dever himself makes several further observations which are also potentially relevant as social evidence. He observes that an early concentration of Israelite settlements east of the highland watershed suggests a strategy to maintain political independence from the city-states. When he notes the proliferation of village silos and storage pits in the highlands, Dever concludes that the villages were not trading with the cities. But should he not have gone on to recognize that the village producers were using local storage facilities to keep what they produced under their own control? It seems to me that these are archaeological materials that a paradigm of radical social change, with its stress on difference, can illuminate—in contrast to Dever's paradigm of symbiosis which, because it underscores sameness, lacks the power to interpret.

Perhaps the fundamental reason for Dever's hesitancy to adopt a covering social theory is that he is dubious that it can guard itself against "forced" explanations "imposed" on the past. The more comprehensive the theory, the more he fears it will wander from the archaeological data attesting to what happened "on the ground." In his view, both the Deuteronomistic theological constructs and my Marxist social-analytic constructs are guilty of making "rhetorical" and "ideological" judgments about early Israel. Within Dever's rhetorical quip, "Who would want to be a Marxist today?" there is a valid question whose answer is straightforwardly as follows: "Anyone would want to be a Marxist who finds that Marxist social theory has more utility for understanding society than other social theoretical options."

Nonetheless, Dever knows that he cannot escape some form of explanatory theory, so for the moment he settles on the symbiosis construct as the "safest" option, presumably because it does not claim too much, even though it makes only a bare start toward clarifying the seminal points in early Israel's social structure and process.

It seems to me that none of us dealing in Israelite origins will be able to formulate a theory "big" enough to make sense of multifaceted early Israel unless we "force the issue" by offering hypotheses within theoretical frameworks that we constantly submit to the available evidence and revise in the give-and-take of scholarly discourse. I choose to force the issue by positing that there was social conflict in ancient societies and that this conflict is not something Marxist method invents but rather uncovers and clarifies, always of course with reference to the specific social-historical evidence for each ancient situation. In other words, my theoretical gamble is that the conflict of class interests in ancient Canaan is the most important key to understanding how Israel arose and took the shape that it did. The basis for evaluating scholarly proposals of this sort is not whether the source of the method employed is a currently popular one, nor is it whether the early Israelites thought about things within the same theoretical framework as scholars do today, since clearly they did not think in any of our critical scientific categories, whether literary, historical, religious, psychological or sociological. The sole basis of theory assessment is this: Does the social explanation offered make more sense of all the relevant evidence—always construed in context—than does any other theory treating the same range of social data?

Realistically, how can any single scholar hope to thoroughly explore and evaluate the adequacy of a complex cross-field theory treating several classes of evidence? One can only proceed by constant reference to the input of other scholars, both in formulating theory and in evaluating theory within a feedback loop of ongoing discourse.[5] This means that biblical and extra-biblical textual scholars, archaeologists, historians of institutions and ideas, and social theorists need to be in regular communication. Symposia and volumes of the kind that Biblical Archaeology Society has initiated in this instance are vital to the multidisciplinary nature of the task, but they work properly only when *all* the relevant scholarly competencies are represented. The social theoretical weakness of Dever's chapter—otherwise so admirable in matters archaeological—is not a personal fault but a structural flaw of atomized scholarly inquiry. The only way to correct that situation is to be sure that any discussion of these issues in a public forum includes the articulate voice of someone versed in how social theory can be used to elucidate early Israel's social history.

ENDNOTES

1. Robert B. Coote and Keith Whitelam, *Emergence of Early Israel in Historical Perspective* (Sheffield, UK: Almond Press, 1987); Coote, *Early Israel. A New Horizon* (Minneapolis, MN: Fortress Press, 1990).

2. James W. Flanagan, *David's Social Drama. A Hologram of Israel's Early Iron Age* (Sheffield, UK: Almond Press, 1988).

3. Neils P. Lemche, *Early Israel. Anthropological and Historical Studies on the Israelite Society Before the Monarchy* (Leiden: Brill, 1985); *Ancient Israel. A New History of Israelite Society* (Sheffield, UK: JSOT Press, 1988).

4. William H. Stiebing, Jr., *Out of the Desert: Archaeology and the Exodus/Conquest Narratives* (Buffalo, NY: Prometheus Books, 1989).

5. For further description of how social data might be collected, categorized and synthesized en route to hypothesis building, see Norman K. Gottwald, "Method and Hypothesis in Reconstructing the Social History of Early Israel," in *Eretz Israel* 24 (Malamat volume), forthcoming.

ADAM ZERTAL
University of Haifa

Invitcd to respond to Professor Dever, I feel the need once again to put the facts on the table, although I feel I've already been in this opera. The facts have been discovered, analyzed and published. Has anybody been listening?

If Mt. Ebal is a picnic area, as Professor Dever jokingly suggests, it is the first ever identified as such. However, religious feasts were known as mass picnics: There meat was eaten, wine drunk, music played and animals sacrificed. Indeed, I have written that Mt. Ebal was a place where pilgrims came. But is it necessary to put the facts on paper again (see my response to Aharon Kempinski,* and my full report on the site)?[1]

Nevertheless, I will again remind Professor Dever of the facts:

1. The Mt. Ebal site is located on a high, isolated and remote place, typical of a cultic high place (as recognized by Michael Coogan[2] and others).

2. There was no evidence of daily living or houses at the site during stratum IB. The only structure there at the time was the altar (or, if you wish, the central building), with its courts, ramps, etc.

3. No architectural parallels whatsoever are known to the central building, apart from my literary comparisons in the Bible, the Mishnah and other sources describing such an altar. It is typical that Professor Dever never even tries to cope with the central structure's details and to explain what it is—if not an altar.

4. The bones excavated at the site are very different from any other Bronze or Iron Age bone inventory—whether comparing species, burning, concentration of bones, etc. You simply have to read my report, Professor Dever. Everything is there. (By the way, the bones were not in jars but in layers—read the report, pp. 114-115!)

5. In the area of the altar were more than a hundred installations with offerings—vessels, jewelry, etc. This is an unparalleled

---

* Adam Zertal, "Has Joshua's Altar Been Found on Mt. Ebal?" *Biblical Archaeology Review,* January/February 1985, and "How Can Kempinski Be So Wrong?" *Biblical Archaeology Review,* January/February 1986.

phenomenon in any other Iron Age I (1200-1000 B.C.E.) site, but it is well known in Bronze Age cult sites and in biblical traditions.

All this has led Israeli and non-Israeli archaeologists to agree on the cultic character of the site, if not to the conclusion that the central building is an altar. I will quote only Amihai Mazar, who Dever has properly identified as "one of the leading younger Israeli archaeologists today": "Zertal may be wrong in the details of his interpretation, but it is tempting to accept his view concerning the basic cultic nature of the site and its possible relationship to the biblical tradition."[3]

As for the "pottery trail," I still think that the settlement process and population movements can be—and should be—based on pottery statistics collected in a surface survey. The assumption that surface pottery represents archaeological periods buried in the site is the basis of all archaeological surveys. I simply took one further step. My theory is that surface pottery may hint—since archaeology is not an exact science—at the foundation date of a given site. My percentages or quantities may be inaccurate, but I could find no logical argument, in Dever's words, against my basic theory. In our survey we did indeed find three consecutive-dating cooking pots in a series of sites from the Jordan Valley westward. Even if the percentages can be interpreted in different ways, the basic facts do not change: the earliest sites are in the east, and the later in the west. If this does not indicate a gradual movement of the settlers, I just don't understand what it means.

Professor Dever appears, these days, in a new metamorphosis. He is now an enthusiastic Mendenhallist. I am not against this. I believe Professor George Mendenhall made some important points and surely pressed all of us to rethink and reevaluate; this is a valuable contribution. But I still believe a balanced scholarly attitude requires us to take into account all the facts, even those that do not conform to our own previously accepted ideas.

It is not by chance that not a single archaeologist has responded seriously to my scientific report on Mt. Ebal. It is not by chance that a serious congress has never been convened to address openly the Mt. Ebal finds, even though many less important matters have been discussed. The reason is that Mt. Ebal presents hard evidence for the existence of an early Israelite cult place, presumably related to the biblical account of Deuteronomy 27 and Joshua 8:30-35. The reason is that if Mt. Ebal so powerfully corroborates the Bible, some of the highly sophisticated theories based on ongoing intellectual speculation (without really examining the field data) will have to go back to square one.

You may lead the horse to the trough, but you can't force him to drink. My finds are just facts, and archaeologists, like other beings, sometimes don't like to be bothered with facts. I think the facts are there. I am not the first in the history of science to stand isolated; it is unpleasant to be alone and antiestablishment. But as I am not the first, so I shall not be the last. It's all a question of time and patience. A balanced view will eventually be adopted.

ENDNOTES

1. Adam Zertal, "An Early Iron Age Cultic Site on Mt. Ebal: Excavation Seasons 1982-1987," *Tel Aviv* 13-14 (1986-1987), pp. 105-165.

2. Michael Coogan, "Of Cults and Cultures: Reflections on the Interpretation of Archaeological Evidence," *Palestine Exploration Quarterly* (January 1987), pp. 1-8. See also Hershel Shanks, "Two Early Israelite Cult Sites Now Questioned," *Biblical Archaeology Review*, January/February 1988, pp. 48-52.

3. Amihai Mazar, *Archaeology of the Land of the Bible* (New York: Doubleday, 1990), p. 350.

Dever's Reply to Finkelstein, Gottwald and Zertal

This reply to the responses of Finkelstein, Gottwald and Zertal
to my talk on the emergence of early Israel must be brief,
because my presentation was meant for a "popular" symposium, not a technical discussion among a few specialist scholars.
Furthermore, I have addressed elsewhere in print nearly all the issues
that my critics have raised; those interested in the details may pursue
the controversies there (see the notes to my chapter, p. 56).

1. *Israel Finkelstein.* Let me reply serially to the three "pillars"
that Finkelstein says my synthesis rests on.

A. *Technology.* Finkelstein seems to think that I believe that
cistern-hewing and terrace-building were entirely new and "resulted"
(his word) in the new hill-country settlements. But I have repeatedly
disavowed such functionalist, mechanistic explanations of Israelite
origins. I have argued instead that such technologies, now developed
to their fullest, *facilitated* the agricultural movement that opened the
highland frontiers to new, more intensive settlement. Cisterns certainly go back to the Middle Bronze Age, as I showed in *Gezer IV*
(Annual of the Nelson Glueck School of Biblical Archaeology, 1986).
Terrace walls may also be attested sporadically in pre-Iron Age con-
texts. But *systematic* terrace-agriculture was not practiced on a large
scale before the Iron Age, as far as we now know. (The article in
Levant cited by Finkelstein describes only one possible Early Bronze
Age terrace wall, stating that the main terrace systems at Sataf are
Roman and Byzantine.)

B. *Ceramic continuity/discontinuity.* Finkelstein downplays the
continuity between the ceramic repertoires of Late Bronze IIB urban
Canaanite sites and his early Iron I "Israelite" sites. I invite the
reader simply to compare the rich, exhaustively documented 13th-
to 12th-century B.C.E. pottery *corpus* at Gezer (which no scholar
thinks an Israelite site) with Finkelstein's late 13th- to 12th-century
stratum III at Israelite 'Izbet Sartah.[1] Finkelstein cannot really argue
that the forms and decorations are different, only that the *percentages* differ. Of course we are dealing, on the one hand, with large

urban sites with a good deal of industrial and trade activity (thus Philistine pottery at Gezer) and, on the other hand, with small, rural agricultural activities (thus more large storage jars and cooking pots at Finkelstein's sites). Finkelstein fails to cite Gloria London's important article, which shows, as I suggested, that such differing percentages point mostly to differing urban and rural lifestyles of what is basically the same "Canaanite" population.[2]

Finkelstein argues that, in any case, ceramic continuity/discontinuity can demonstrate only "environmental and socioeconomic conditions," not the origins of peoples. Would he say the same thing of *Philistine* pottery, which is the basic clue to the Aegean origins of these peoples? Most archaeologists and anthropologists I know operate on the basic assumption that "pottery is our most sensitive medium for perceiving shared aesthetic traditions, in the sense that they define ethnic groups, for recognizing culture contact and culture change, and for following migration and trade patterns."[3]

The close similarities—indeed, almost identical late-13th- and early-12th-century B.C.E. repertoires—strongly support my Canaanite-Israelite symbiosis model. To prove his sedentarized nomads model, Finkelstein would have to produce at least *some* new 12th-century pottery forms that could have come out of an earlier or contemporary local pastoral-nomadic culture—such as the well-known, handmade Negbite pottery of nonsedentary peoples in the Negev, found alongside the typical Iron Age forms.

C. *Settlement patterns and demography.* Finkelstein argues that I am wrong in seeing the early Iron I villages as representing the first effective, large-scale settlement of a region that had been relatively sparsely occupied earlier. For data on earlier settlement patterns, he cites only the "forthcoming" publication of his own surveys in the *Bulletin of the American Schools of Oriental Research* (*BASOR*), which I had not seen when I wrote, and in the *Israel Exploration Journal* 41 (1991). Now that I have seen the *BASOR* article—and it is a most valuable piece of research—I note that Finkelstein has mapped 126 Early Bronze sites and 248 Middle Bronze sites in the hill country (p. 42). But even if I had had that information, there is nothing in this article that quantifies the size, character or estimated population of these pre-Iron Age settlements. So how can we compare? Even Finkelstein says that "a large portion of the population during these

two periods (and in the Iron Age) were local pastoralists who became sedentary" (p. 43; again citing his forthcoming article). My
main point was not that there was no pre-Iron I settlement in the
hill country, but rather that the sharp increase in sites from Late
Bronze to Iron I represents a *major* demographic change, one that
reflects a sizable influx of new settlers. And this point both Larry
Stager and I have taken from Finkelstein's *own* survey data in his
1985 thesis and in his 1988 book *The Archaeology of the Israelite
Settlement.* Thus we agree that the "proto-Israelites" were newcomers, and in relatively large numbers. We disagree only on where
those newcomers came *from.*

I welcome new survey data and analysis, but it is not likely that
it will change the present consensus that early Iron I in the hill
country represents a significant demographic shift. As for Finkelstein's
stress on the necessity for *long-term* settlement history, I have been
calling for that in print for a decade; even some of Finkelstein's
language seems borrowed from me.

I could easily reply to a number of other aspects of Finkelstein's
closing four-point agenda for future research. While his critique
often overstates the case, or is shockingly wrong (such as the statement that I "follow the biblical tradition" of "Israel as a unique
phenomenon"), there are many sound and valuable observations
here. But Finkelstein's main point, his overriding thesis in *all* his
recent published works (as well as, apparently, in unpublished works)
is that the majority, if not all, of the proto-Israelites were former
local pastoral nomads, now sedentarized. He cites again, as his *only*
evidence, the Bedouin-like "tent circle" plan of 'Izbet Sartah stratum
III; he does *not* cite, however, the important refutation of his entire
argument by his *own field supervisor* at 'Izbet Sartah, Zvi Lederman
of Harvard, whose article "Nomads They Never Were" (*Society of
Biblical Literature Abstracts* 1990) is devastating to Finkelstein's case.
Nor does Finkelstein quote from my review of his book in *Bulletin of
the American Schools of Oriental Research* (284 [1991], pp. 77-90)
(although he does cite it), where I show, on the basis of his own
anthropologist's and paleobotanical/zoological reports, that the
economy and society of 'Izbet Sartah appear to reflect *long-standing*
sedentarization. Zvi Lederman has given me permission to quote
him on what has been my own strong suspicion all along: Finkelstein

has absolutely *no* hard archaeological data for his notion of a pastoral-nomadic derivation for early Israel. It is a provocative theory, and I myself have suggested that *some* of the proto-Israelites may have been former pastoralists. But there is as yet no archaeological proof whatsoever—and much evidence to the contrary.

In my view, Finkelstein is dangerously wedded to a theory that is either based on Alt and Noth's peaceful infiltration model of the 1930s, or else one that comes from the long-outmoded notion in biblical scholarship of a "nomadic ideal" in the Bible—a sort of "nostalgia for a biblical past that never was." I have the highest regard for Israel Finkelstein's pioneering research on the Israelite settlement; and I can claim to be one of the first to recognize and promote in America his absolutely fundamental work. But his nomadic origins model is too idiosyncratic to command much support so far, much less to be presented as a consensus in a popular symposium.

2. *Norman Gottwald.* On many occasions I have quoted and praised my colleague and friend Norman Gottwald, whose cumulative work is without doubt one of the handful of truly original contributions to 20th-century biblical scholarship. If he has now moved beyond some of what I would call the "Hegelian excess baggage" of his 1979 peasant revolt and egalitarian models, that simply enhances the value of his always-sensitive appreciation of early Israel. But in all candor, I do not see that a less-ambitious communitarian model is better. What does it *really* say, except that early Israel was a "community"? What society about which we know anything was *not*? Even specifying this, as Gottwald does, in terms of "free agrarians," or in terms of "agricultural surpluses" and "intertribal networking," is not especially helpful. The problem is that (1) such socioeconomic aspects characterize *many* ethnic groups or cultures, not just ancient Israel; (2) overall, the resultant portrait of early Israel is very idealistic, almost utopian; and (3) in any case, there is little *archaeological* evidence, nor can much be expected. In short, here is another theory that, like Finkelstein's, only describes; it does not really explain—which is the ultimate goal of all historical and archaeo-anthropological inquiry.

Gottwald complains that my more minimalistic symbiosis model also does not explain; it does not answer the question, how and why was early Israel *different*? But that is just the point: My model is deliberately simple and descriptive; and it does not claim to be "explanatory," because none of us at present *can* explain early Israel. Gottwald, like Mendenhall, looks to ideology for an explanation—in this case Yahwism. But I have repeatedly warned that archaeology deals primarily with *material* culture, and at best with only some of the behavior that produced material things; it is poorly suited, if at all, for recouping the *ideas* behind human actions. Of course they are, or were, there; but in all due modesty, I as an archaeologist leave that to the speculation of theologians, philosophers and other theorists. Gottwald urges what anthropologists often call "more robust" theory, while I prefer more archaeological *data* and only the minimum theory necessary. I would remind my colleague that in the field of formal logic, it is a fundamental principle that the preferable theory is always the "most parsimonious," i.e., the simplest theory that will accommodate the known facts—in this case, the only contemporary "facts" being the archaeological ones (the biblical texts being all later, usually much later). As for my quip about "no one wanting to be a Marxist today," that may have sounded unkind, but it was not intended to be. Gottwald's Marxist sentiments arise, I believe, out of a deep, honest and courageous commitment to social causes that is entirely admirable and, perhaps, to a Liberation Theology that many will find attractive. But two facts seem clear to me: (1) "Class conflict," while universal, is neither very visible in the archaeological record, nor is it adequate to explain the emergence of ancient Israel; (2) Marxist (or, more properly, neo-Marxist) paradigms in anthropology and archaeology (probably in social theory, as well) were on their way out a decade ago, long before the collapse of the Soviet bloc discredited Marxist theory in general. Gottwald is a formidable interpreter of early Israel, but in his neo-Marxist orientation he stands almost alone among biblical scholars in the English-speaking world. That was my only rationale in not dealing more substantively with his views in a popular symposium—that, plus the fact that the one paper he cites for his changing opinions is unpublished, so of course I have not seen it. I look forward to it eagerly! Incidentally, as for the works he cites by such scholars as Coote and Whitelam, Flanagan, Lemche, etc., I not only have read them extensively, but own them, have reviewed them and most recently have cited them, along with many others, in Gottwald's own 1992 *festschrift, The Politics of Exegesis* (Pilgrim, 1992). He says that on recent theory I am "at sea." The point is that we *all* are at this moment: He simply charts a course to a distant and dangerous harbor, while I, as an archaeologist, perhaps seek a safer and more secure port in the storm.

3. *Adam Zertal.* I find it difficult to respond to Zertal. His insistence that the "facts" speak for themselves, if only *someone* would pay attention to him, is rather sad. I have read his reports; but like all the other archaeologists I know, I remain skeptical that Mt. Ebal is a shrine, much less "Joshua's altar." Since he admits that he stands alone, I do not think a reply is necessary.

Concerning his "survey statistics" and the proof that these indicate an east-west movement of settlers, I simply repeat that the fact that he has *any* of his early "Type A" cooking pots at western sites— as he does—disproves his basic theory. The western sites may be smaller, or the early sherds fewer by reason of the accidents of surface pickup, but these sites are clearly *founded* just as early as the easternmost sites. Virtually everyone concedes that the westernmost site of *all*—'Izbet Sartah—was certainly founded in the 13th century B.C.E. and is among the earliest. I simply ask again: Where is the *evidence* for the supposed east-to-west movement? It seems obvious to me that Zertal has been seduced by the later biblical notion of a mass migration from Transjordan—against *all* the current archaeological evidence. This tendency is what some of his own Israeli colleagues have labeled "secular fundamentalism"—no less dangerous and misleading than the biblical kind. Even if Zertal were proven correct, it would still not change the "indigenous Canaanite" consensus; Transjordan in antiquity was simply eastern Palestine or Canaan.

The literal biblical story of an Exodus from Egypt, and a subsequent pan-Israelite conquest of Canaan, can no longer be salvaged, for all the wishful thinking in the world. What actually happened was much more complicated, and we are only beginning to understand it, thanks largely to recent archaeological discoveries.

In conclusion, I would remind readers that a popular presentation such as mine inevitably oversimplifies, and may even be misleading at certain points. Regarding the need for forums more scholarly than this format, where all points of view can be presented and fully documented, I agree entirely with Gottwald. Perhaps I may point out that I was the first scholar to open up the scholarly discussion in America to the general public, in the 1987 national meetings of the Society of Biblical Literature/American Schools of Oriental Research. And among the scholars that I invited to participate were Robert Coote and Keith Whitelam, Israel Finkelstein, Lawrence Stager and Norman Gottwald—all mentioned in the exchange of views here. That discussion continues and expands.

ENDNOTES

1. See, for example, Israel Finkelstein, *The Archaeology of the Israelite Settlement* (Jerusalem: Israel Exploration Society, 1988), fig. 20.

2. Gloria London, "A Comparison of Two Contemporaneous Lifestyles of the Late Second Millennium B.C.," *Bulletin of the American Schools of Oriental Research* 273 (1987), pp. 37-55.

3. R.W. Ehrich, ed., *Chronologies in Old World Archaeology* (Chicago: Univ. of Chicago Press, 1965), pp. vii, viii.

I

f you think the issue of the Israelite settlement is tough, it's nothing compared to the Exodus. Now the Exodus, that's a real tough one. We are very fortunate today to have with us to discuss the Exodus, Baruch Halpern. Baruch Halpern is a major younger scholar. He is not yet 40 years old. He has been at York University in Canada, but has just accepted a professorship at Penn State University in Pennsylvania, where he will form a whole new department of religious studies. All of today's speakers, except myself, have their Ph.D.'s from Harvard. Maybe that's not so good, we are bringing you a Harvard perspective. Baruch graduated summa cum laude *and his Ph.D. dissertation was accepted with highest honors. If I were to read Baruch's curriculum vitae we would be here all day. He is the author of several important scholarly books, one called* The Constitution of the Monarchy in Israel, *another entitled* The Emergence of Israel in Canaan *and still another called* The First Historians. *He is widely known as a brilliant and insightful speaker, as well as a writer. I'm sure you'll enjoy him and learn from him. It's a pleasure to introduce my friend Baruch Halpern.—H.S.*

BARUCH HALPERN

The Exodus from Egypt: Myth or Reality?

T hank you very much. Hershel began his talk with the comment that you could accept whatever he said unequivocally. I wish I could say the same thing about his introduction. (Laughter.)

Under what circumstances did Romulus and Remus found Rome? What was the role of Hercules, or Jason and the Argonauts, in creating a unified Mycenaean consciousness? If you can answer those questions, you are ready to tackle the issue of the Exodus. For our accounts of the Exodus reflect the prehistory of the Israelite nation, or, perhaps, of some part of it.

The closest parallel to the Book of Exodus in the ancient West is Homer's *Odyssey*. Both are stories of migration—of identity suspended until the protagonist—Odysseus or Israel—reaches a home. Neither account records events of the sort that are likely to have left marks in the archaeological record, or even in contemporaneous monuments. At both ends of the journey, though, in Egypt and

Israel or at Troy and Ithaca, the narrative can be said to reflect local conditions. In both cases, our sources reflect long-term oral transmission, followed by authoritative codification in writing. In both cases, there is evidence of that peculiar process of oral transmission in which the story is renegotiated with each separate audience each time it is told.[1] Each story reflects a healthy admixture of fancy with whatever is being recalled.

The *Odyssey* is the story of an individual at odds with sorceresses, one-eyed cannibals and sirens—very much like a metaphor for the journey of a social welfare bill through the legislature. The implausibility of the story occasions no great difficulty: Augustine tells us that the *Odyssey* was taught as gospel in the Greek world of his day; it is basically a piece of children's literature. So, in its way, is the story of the Exodus.

But the Exodus is not the story of an individual; it is the story of a nation. It is the historical myth of an entire people, a focal point for national identity. The Exodus story was to the ancient Israelite what the stories of the Pilgrims and the Revolutionary War are to Americans. At a deep level, in fact, our American fathers modeled their notions of identity and history on the Exodus.[2]

The Exodus coded certain common values into the culture. All Israel shared the background of the ancestors—all Israel had been slaves in Egypt. Whatever one's biological ancestry, to be an Israelite meant that one's ancestors—spiritual or emotive or collective ancestors—had risen from Egypt to conquer Canaan. *YHWH** liberated the Israelites from Egypt and executed a covenant with them. The covenant stipulated that, in return for their emancipation *and* for the gift of the land of Canaan, Israel would worship *YHWH* and obey his law. In Near Eastern culture, a sovereign who saved his subjects from ruin *and gave them land* merited loyalty. This nexus furnished the myth of the Passover, celebrated every spring as the green wheat broke ground. This was the story of how Israel came to be, and how it came into possession of Canaan. For without the conquest of Canaan, the Exodus would have been without a point.

The earliest Israelite Passover ritual already incorporated the

---

* *YHWH* is the personal name of the Israelite God, often spelled Yahweh, although we don't know how exactly the final syllable was pronounced. The four-letter consonantal form *YHWH* is known as the tetragrammaton.

pretense that the participants were in transition from Egypt to Israel, from bondage to freedom: The unleavened bread they ate was (and is) the "bread of affliction," the unleavened bread that their ancestors ate on leaving Egypt. And the roasted lamb they ate was the stuff of rugged campfires; it reflected the absence of basic amenities—since in civilized settings, meat was always boiled.[3] The ritual of the Passover, in sum, always presupposed the threshold location of the celebrant, between bondage and freedom, between Egypt and Canaan, in the realm of the uncivilized.

The difference between the early Israelite celebration and the Jewish festival is this: The Jewish celebrant in the Diaspora expresses hopes for national reintegration; the ancient Israelites knew, from the bleatings of the flocks and from the greening of the landscape all around them, that the festival would leave them in possession of the land of Canaan.

Yet modern scholarship divorces the Exodus from its completion in the conquest. For the relation of the Exodus to Israel's settlement of Canaan is no longer as clear as it was to the Israelites of the Iron Age.* Neither the date of the Exodus nor the duration of Israel's sojourn in Egypt can now be ascertained with any confidence. Consequently, we cannot accurately gauge the interval between the Exodus and the emergence of Israel in Canaan. More the pity: to the Israelite of the Iron Age, the events were all but simultaneous; this is the reason that the Book of Joshua locates Israel's entry into Canaan at the time of the Passover (Joshua 4:19, 5:10-11).

The *historical* uncertainty arises from the nature of our sources, and of the events reported. Endless generations of oral recital have made themselves felt in shaping the literature. The accounts—of J, E, P, D** and other sources—differ in detail.[4] And the story of the Exodus is so central to Israelite identity that changes in that identity almost unconsciously registered in the evolution of the story. Nevertheless, behind the Exodus story events can be discerned that, unlike

---

* Iron I is the period of Israel's emergence in Canaan, biblically the period of the Judges—1200-1000 B.C.E. Iron II is the period of the Israelite monarchy, both the United Monarchy and the Divided Monarchy, and ends with the Babylonian conquest of Jerusalem in 586 B.C.E.
** J, E, P and D are the names scholars give to the four principal textual strands that comprise the Pentateuch—J for Yahwist (Jahwist in German), E for Elohist, P for priestly code and D for Deuteronomist. JE, used below, designates an early combination of the two. R designates the redactor, or editor, who combined strands.

those of the patriarchal narratives, can be termed historical in scale.

First, to the matter of dates. The Bible basically offers us a choice of various dates for the Exodus. First Kings 6:1 places the building of Solomon's Temple 480 years after the Exodus, which would put the Exodus around 1450 B.C.E., smack in the reign of Thutmosis III, the Augustus of the Egyptian empire. The Bible also tells us that the Israelites grew from a clan of 72 males to a mighty "mixed multitude" of around 600,000 adult males during their stay in Egypt—the number is from the P source (Genesis 46:8-27; Exodus 1:5, 12:37; Numbers 1:18,46-47, 26:4,51). Other sources recall a stay of four generations (Genesis 15:16 [J or R_{JE}]; Exodus 6:16-27 [P]), over the course of which such a population explosion seems implausible; or of 400 years (Genesis 15:13 [R_{JEP}?]; cf. Exodus 12:40-41 [P]).

At the end of the sojourn in Egypt, under the pharaoh of the oppression, the Israelites built the store-cities of Ramses and Pithom. Ramses was rebuilt as a capital in the reign of Ramesses II, in the 13th century B.C.E.* The pharaoh of the Exodus, who succeeded the pharaoh of the oppression (Exodus 2:23), and who seems to drown during the Exodus (Exodus 14:6-8,10,27-30), would then be Merneptah, Ramesses' son and successor. Unfortunately, according to a hieroglyphic inscription known as the Merneptah Stele, or the Israel Stele, Merneptah already knew of an Israel living in Asia in the fifth year of his reign, around 1230 B.C.E. Even assuming that the pharaoh of the Exodus didn't drown, Israel cannot have left in the first year of Merneptah and then wandered in the wilderness for 40 years before turning up in Canaan in his fifth year.

So either one must divorce the Exodus from the conquest, as I shall try to do a bit later on, or one must remove the reference to the store-cities. The alternative, lately in vogue, is to claim that the Israelites built not Ramses, but the town of Avaris, the ancient predecessor of Ramses. But any such activity would have to be located at least 150 years before 1450 B.C.E.—in which case, the pharaoh of the Exodus will not have been the immediate successor to the pharaoh

---

* The dates for Ramesses II are variously given as: 1304-1238 B.C.E. on the high chronology, 1290-1224 B.C.E. on the middle chronology and 1279-1213 B.C.E. on the low chronology. I like the high chronology. However, this means that the date for Merneptah's Stele would be about 1230 B.C.E. rather than 1207 as cited by our other speakers today.

of the oppression.

In short, one or another aspect of the biblical account will have to be jettisoned. Now, the question is, how shall we choose which aspects to retain?

Not so long ago, had you asked my younger daughter what animal she most fervently wished as a pet, she'd have answered, "a unicorn." The actual evidence concerning the Exodus resembles the evidence for the unicorn. We have replicas, even cuddly reproductions, but we never seem to lay our hands on the real thing. To put it in a different light, what we have are Israelite writings from the Iron Age that reflect back on Egypt and Canaan in the Bronze Age.* So, the first question is, what were Israel's ideas about Israelite prehistory in the Bronze Age? What did the Israelites know about the Bronze Age, and what role did they think their ancestors played in it? Oddly enough, the way to get at the Exodus is to focus, not on all the contradictory and unstable details in the biblical text, but on the conceptual framework within which the Israelite authors furnished those details.

The place to start is with the Book of Genesis, which tells us that Israel (Jacob)** descended to Egypt in a time of famine and found that his son Joseph, who had been sold into slavery, had risen to be vizier there. Where in Egyptian history does this story belong?

Semitic slaves are attested in Egypt from the beginning of the second millennium on down. The Amarna letters† clarify the context: Whenever warfare or drought wracked Asia, townsmen in Canaan sold their families to Egypt in exchange for grain.[5] Sometimes these slaves rose to positions of considerable prominence in Egypt, often to major power.[6] The universal experience of Canaanites, in other words, was that in times of famine, Canaanites were sent down to Egypt. And when the Canaanites were pastoralists, it was to the land of Goshen they went—the area where the Israelites settled.

---

* The Bronze Age is divided into Early, Middle and Late; it extends from about 3000 to 1200 B.C.E. The dates generally given for the Late Bronze Age are 1550 to 1200 B.C.E. The transition is probably to be dated from 1590-1530 B.C.E. or so. Transitions from period to period take time, and don't occur in a single year or even in a single decade.

**Jacob's name was changed to Israel at Penuel (Genesis 32:25-33).

† The Amarna letters are a set of documents sent to or from Pharaoh Amenhotep III or Amenhotep IV. They are so called because the bulk of them were discovered at Amenhotep IV's capital, Tell el-Amarna in Egypt. For the most part, this archive consists of correspondence from Egyptian vassals in Asia.

This is the background against which the myth of Israel's descent into Egypt must be viewed.

Earlier, Hershel Shanks remarked on the history of the Hyksos in Egypt. Is the Joseph story set before that time, in the Egyptian Middle Kingdom,* when Semitic immigration into Egypt produced records of Semitic slaves and even Semitic officials in the Delta? At that time, the pharaohs based themselves in Thebes, some 350 miles south of the Nile Delta, so this creates a problem.

Does the Joseph story belong in the Hyksos era, when Semites rose to be nomarchs (kings of districts) and even pharaohs? These were the rulers of the XVth Dynasty;** the Egyptian priest, Manetho,† interprets the term Hyksos[7] to mean "shepherd kings." These Semitic "invaders" of Egypt—the invasion itself may have taken the form of a longstanding immigration into the Delta—expanded from their base in the Delta—at Avaris (Tell ed-Dab'a on the Pelusiac branch of the Nile)—to control Egypt as a whole for about a century. Ahmose, the founder of the XVIIIth Dynasty, expelled the Hyksos sometime around 1565 B.C.E., and relocated the capital again at Thebes.[8] Does the Joseph story belong to the period after that expulsion, the period of the XVIIIth and XIXth Dynasties, when Egypt held sway not only over Canaan but over Asia as far as the Euphrates?

Shanks notes that some scholars have associated Joseph's rise with the Hyksos. This was the tradition related in antiquity. Manetho, a priest who wrote a history of Egypt in the third century B.C.E., placed Joseph's entry into Egypt and his rise in the early part of the reign of the Hyksos king, Apophis. The Hyksos were expelled, and then Moses called them back to help the later Israelites escape from Egypt.

To ask whether Manetho corroborates the Joseph story is to invert the actual relationship: Manetho relied on the Bible, probably at secondhand, since he concluded that the Israelites were lepers (cf. Numbers 11) and that Moses was Osarsiph, priest of On (cf. Joseph, who married the daughter, we are told, of a priest of On). Yet the

* The dating of the Middle Kingdom is disputed, but ran from the late third millennium to about 1700-1650 B.C.E.
** The XVth Dynasty ruled Egypt from about 1650 to 1550 B.C.E.
† We know of Manetho only from writings of his quoted by Josephus, a Jewish historian of the first century C.E., and by the church fathers Eusebius and Africanus (the latter preserved by Syncellus in the ninth century). Manetho wrote in the third century B.C.E.

Hyksos interlude impressed itself indelibly in Egyptian memory. Pharaoh Kamose, predecessor of Ahmose who expelled the Hyksos, accused them of widespread destruction, and there are indications of famine in the period.[9] Egyptians accused the Hyksos in hindsight of neglecting all the gods but Seth, and of imposing heavy taxes. Manetho echoes these claims, and complains that the Hyksos accumulated grain at their capital Avaris and enslaved the population.

Joseph is said to have imposed a harsh regime of taxation in Egypt to accumulate grain to weather an approaching famine.[10] Genesis is suggestive: "To this day," it claims, Egypt's peasants have the status of tenant farmers, and must pay 20 percent of their produce to their landlord, the pharaoh (Genesis 47:18-26 [J]). The text thus deflects complaints about Hyksos oppression: Joseph introduced the system in order to avert a worse catastrophe, starvation. Joseph's name in Egypt reflects this interpretation—resisting any convincing Egyptian etymology, the name should be understood as a portmanteau of Semitic and Egyptian: ṣaphnat pa-'anḥ, the "cool north wind of life." Like the north wind relieving the oppressive heat down the Nile Valley, Joseph is the Semite blowing in from the north who gives new life to Egypt.

What's more, the Bible claims that no subsequent pharaoh has reformed Joseph's tax. The Egyptian regime in the Iron Age is the legatee of Joseph's policies. This claim of continuity between Hyksos Egypt and Iron Age Egypt reflects the exposure of Israelite merchants and diplomats to Egyptian culture, as we shall see.

The portrayal of the Israelites as "shepherds" in Genesis is no coincidence either: The Egyptians remembered the Hyksos as "shepherd-kings." Joseph is introduced as a shepherd, destined to be a ruler.[11] The Israelites are associated with herds, and when they enter Egypt are settled in Goshen, based on their belief that it furnishes good pasturage.

Some scholars claim that the location of the Israelite herders falsifies the biblical reports. Goshen was the Wadi* Tumilat, just south of the Delta. The natural point of entry for Canaanites bringing flocks into Egypt was through the Wadi Tumilat.[12] But an Egyptian pharaoh of the XVIIIth Dynasty (c. 1575-1318 B.C.E. on the

---

* A wadi is a stream or riverbed that is dry for some part of the year.

high chronology)—after the Hyksos expulsion—would have been 350 miles away, in Thebes. How, then, did Moses, or, for that matter, Joseph, enjoy almost daily contact with the pharaoh?

In one source, Joseph instructs his brothers that they will settle in Goshen, so as to be close to him.[13] The implication is that Joseph, the viceroy, resides near Goshen, in the eastern Delta. In the continuation,[14] Joseph is reconciled to his brothers, "And the sound was heard in the pharaoh's house" (Genesis 45:2). In other words, the pharaonic residence is close to Joseph's, in the Delta. There are several other texts with the same implication.[15] This can only be the case during the period of Hyksos rule in Egypt (c. 1800-1550 B.C.E.). The biblical tradition thus identifies Israel's descent into Egypt with the Hyksos.

The Hyksos capital of Egypt has now been located—at Tell ed-Dabʿa in the eastern Delta, just north of Goshen. Semitic settlement there started by the mid-18th century at the latest.[16] Assume that Joseph worked for the Hyksos: J's idea of a 400-year sojourn places the Exodus under the Ramessides (13th century B.C.E.).

It was just in that era that Ramesses II relocated the capital from Thebes back to Tell ed-Dabʿa. The Ramessides reconstructed the Hyksos capital at Avaris—and called it Ramses; they were conscious of the Hyksos connections.

This same consciousness seems to underlie the biblical accounts, which locate the Israelites in Goshen in the Hyksos and the Ramesside periods. Settlement in Tell ed-Dabʿa persisted into the 11th century B.C.E.[17] So Egyptian memories probably affected Israelite tradition. The author of the J source, after all, was no hillbilly: He was a literate adjutant of the court in Jerusalem, with the historical knowledge of a member of the elite. He simply located the Joseph story in a particular historical milieu, rather than in a vacuum. One of the kings of the XXIst Egyptian Dynasty (c. 1075-948 B.C.E), possibly Solomon's father-in-law (1 Kings 3:1, 9:16), transferred the capital from Ramses to Tanis. The transfer brought innumerable Ramesside and Hyksos monuments to Tanis.[18] So traditions of Ramesside and Hyksos activity just north of Goshen, at Tell ed-Dabʿa, survived into the period when the Israelite court developed formalized relations with Egypt.

The mediation of these Egyptian memories to Israel either

THE HYKSOS CAPITAL of ancient Avaris has now been fixed at Tell ed-Dab'a, just north of Goshen, in the eastern Delta. The Hyksos, a Semitic people from Asia, settled in the area as far back as the mid-18th century B.C.E. Hyksos pharaohs even ruled Egypt for a time. Historian Baruch Halpern notes that if the story of Joseph reflects Hyksos dominance in Egypt and if the figure of 400 years for the Israelite sojourn in Egypt as given in the Bible is correct, then the Exodus would have occurred during the Ramesside dynasty (13th century B.C.E.).

fostered a tradition that Israel's ancestors ruled in the Delta region, or attached itself to such a tradition. At the same time, the presence of the Hyksos monuments at Tanis misled Israelite tradition into the conviction that Tanis, founded in the 11th century, was a Middle Bronze II (1800-1550 B.C.E.) site—hence the claim, in J, that Hebron—a Middle Bronze fortress—was founded seven years before Tanis, and later references to an Exodus setting out from "the plain of Tanis" (Numbers 13:22; on the plain of Tanis, see Psalm 78). Significantly, one of the monuments moved to Tanis was a stele of Ramesses II celebrating the inauguration of the cult of the Hyksos god Seth 400 years earlier.[19] The idea of a four-century span between the Hyksos (and Joseph) and the pharaoh who built the city Ramses

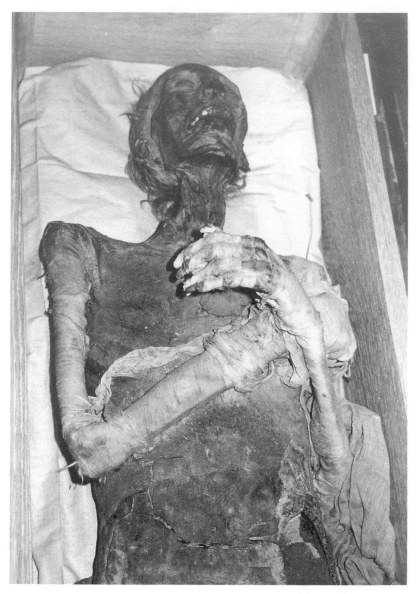

THE MIGHTY RAMESSES II, pharaoh from 1304 to 1238 B.C.E. (on the high chronology used by Halpern), who lived to about 90, is thought by many scholars to have been either the pharaoh of the Exodus or of the oppression (if the latter, the dubious honor of pharaoh of the Exodus would fall to his son Merneptah, whose stele mentioning Israel is shown on p. 18). Ramesses II undertook massive building projects requiring vast amounts of labor, including the relocation of the royal capital to, and the reconstruction of, the old Hyksos capital at Avaris; the site was renamed Ramses.

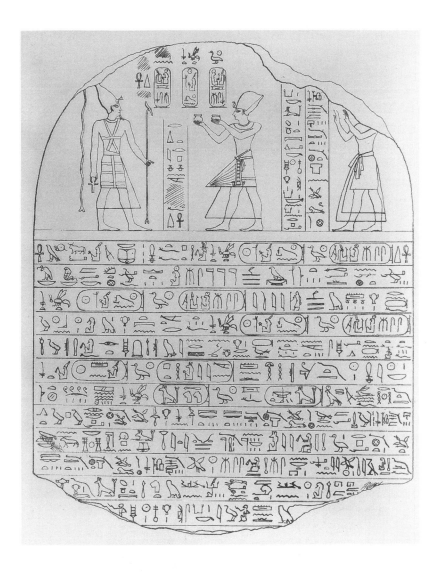

THE FOUR-HUNDRED-YEAR STELE. During the early tenth century B.C.E., an Egyptian pharaoh of the XXIst Dynasty (c. 1075-948 B.C.E.), perhaps Solomon's father-in-law, transferred the capital from Ramses (formerly Avaris) to Tanis. Among the monuments moved in the process was this stele of Ramesses II, which records the inauguration of the cult of the Hyksos god Seth 400 years earlier. Baruch Halpern suggests that this stele, moved at a time when relations between Solomon's court and the Egyptian court were good and when parts of the Bible were being composed in Jerusalem, is responsible for the biblical notion that 400 years separated Joseph (or the Hyksos) and the pharaoh who pressed the Israelites into building the capital city Ramses.

using Israelite labor must be traced, directly or indirectly, to that monument.

Overall, the Joseph story is a reinterpretation of the Hyksos period from an Israelite perspective. Admitting a relationship between Israel and the Hyksos, it affirms that the episode was part of a divine plan to preserve both the Asiatics and the Egyptians. The framework of the Joseph story, then, is plainly apologetic: It offers up the perspective of the despised "Asiatics" against centuries of Egyptian opprobrium. The tradition's date is uncertain, but its most probable time of origin is in the tenth century, under, or just after, Solomon.

So far, we can conclude that Israelite tradition associated the descent into Egypt with the Hyksos period of Middle Bronze IIB-C

JACOB SCARAB. *The connections between the Hyksos period and the Israelite tradition of descent into Egypt has a solid historical basis, Halpern notes. Shown here is a scarab, or beetle-shaped, seal bearing the name Y'qb-HR, the Egyptian transliteration of the Canaanite name "Yaqub" (Jacob). Discovered near Haifa in 1969, the seal has been dated to the 18th century B.C.E. and is thought to have belonged to a Canaanite king named Jacob. This Jacob may have been an ancestor of another Jacob, a Hyksos king who ruled Egypt about a century later. The Bible describes all Israelites as having descended from a Jacob who traveled from Canaan to Egypt during a period of famine.*

(c. 1800-1550 B.C.E.). This association is not limited to the texts about Joseph. Abraham, for example, is thought to have settled in Hebron—which the Israelites knew to be founded on a rich Middle Bronze site.

But are these connections to the Hyksos era purely literary and folkloristic? Two groups of data support the view that the Israelite nexus to the Hyksos has some historicity to it. The first is striking. The name "Jacob" appears on a number of scarabs as the name of at least one Hyksos king.[20] All Israel claims descent from an ancestor named Jacob. The connection between the eponym, Jacob, and the forgotten name of the Hyksos king, in the context, is a tantalizing one.

Second, the names of the patriarchs in Genesis are almost uniformly of a type that most probably derives from the Middle Bronze Age, the Hyksos era. This is true of Isaac, Ishmael, Israel, Joseph and especially Jacob. Names of this type are relatively rare after the Middle Bronze, yet they appear in a high concentration in Israelite ancestral lore. Our inference should be that the ancestral lore has its roots in—that is, the names of the patriarchs derive from—the Middle Bronze Age, the period of the Hyksos.[21] All the indications are that Israelite lore has in fact picked up on a stream of tradition the headwaters of which stem from that time.

Now, what implications does this have for the event of the Exodus? The Bible places this event overtly under Merneptah (c. 1237-1227 B.C.E.), and the oppression under Ramesses II (c. 1304-1238). And there are convincing details: Texts of Ramesses II even refer to construction by captive 'Apiru,[22] an Egyptian term for a type of Semite sometimes encountered in small numbers on military campaigns. This term is probably related to the later Israelite word, "Hebrew" (*'ivri*), used in the Bible to describe Israelite ethnicity to foreigners, and used frequently in the Book of Exodus. But the Egyptian term, "'Apiru," lost its currency by the tenth century. Though the Israelite ethnicon "Hebrew" survived, the juxtaposition of the two similar words may reflect the origins of the Egyptian term in the second millennium B.C.E.

The brickmaking, too, described as part of the oppression, reflects close knowledge of conditions in Egypt. A 15th-century tomb painting depicts Canaanite and Nubian captives making bricks at Thebes. One text even complains about a dearth of straw for

THE 'APIRU. The highlighted area at lower left on this Amarna tablet contains a reference to an 'Apiru leader named Lab'ayyu. "'Apiru" was an Egyptian term for bands of Semitic warriors or brigands who had destabilized numerous locales in Egyptian-dominated Canaan. According to some scholars, the term is related to the later Israelite word 'ivri (Hebrew), used in the Bible to describe the Israelites to other ethnic groups.

brickmaking—a situation encountered by Israel in Egypt.[23] In Canaan, by contrast, straw was not typically an ingredient of mudbrick. Almost every detail in the tradition mirrors conditions under the XIXth Dynasty.[24] Especially, the idea of a sudden rise in forced labor around the time of Ramesses II is entirely consonant with historical reality.[25]

To reoccupy Avaris/Per-Ramses, Ramesses II constructed a dominating palace, lavish temples and ambitious waterworks. He decorated his new capital with statuary and other monuments on a grand scale, almost without end. And, of course, he imported to the new capital the infrastructure to support both the ongoing construction and the government of Egypt.

At the same time, a significant proportion of the population of the Delta, drafted into public construction, was Semitic. Asiatic captives were typically employed in temple construction and other state projects under the XVIIIth Dynasty. But typically, this was in the south.[26] It was the Delta, and especially the eastern Delta, that was an Asiatic cultural preserve.[27] Its potential for labor was first tapped by Ramesses II. Ramesses II built huge public works on a truly massive scale all over Egypt, stamping his name across the landscape from the Delta to Abu Simbel. He made extensive use of forced labor, and no doubt of Semitic slaves, in these enterprises.[28]

However long the Israelites stayed in Egypt, then, the biblical presentation identifies the Exodus with the end of the Late Bronze Age. Ramesses II is the pharaoh of the oppression, in the 13th century B.C.E. The city, (Per-)Ramses, was constructed in the 13th century: Pithom was also occupied at about this time, though its location remains a matter of some controversy.[29] The scale of the Israelite enslavement, too, best matches the time of Ramesses II, when a strong and martial Egypt flourished, and monumental construction in the grand style reached its apogee based in part on exactions in Asia. In fact, if Ramesses II's 400-year stele has inspired the biblical tradition of a 400-year sojourn in Egypt, a conviction that Ramesses II was the pharaoh of the oppression has actually shaped the development of Israel's traditions: The Semites subjected to forced labor in the Delta identified themselves with the traditions of their Hyksos predecessors, against the Egyptian pharaoh; thus Israel came to identify itself with the Hyksos. The nature of the biblical tradition assumes a very reasonable cast if one assumes that behind it is an experience of forced labor in the late XVIIIth or early XIXth Dynasty.

Further, the list of peoples Israel allegedly encountered when *en route* from Egypt to Canaan speaks strongly for an exodus in the same era: Midian, Amalek, Edom, Moab and Ammon (Numbers 13, 14, 20-24). Moab first appears as a nation, organized as such, in the time of Ramesses II. The Edomites first appear as such under Merneptah, the son of Ramesses II, probably in southern Transjordan. Midian and Amalek occupied territory in the southern reaches of Canaan or in the Hejaz in Iron I, just after Merneptah's time, but are unknown either before or after.[30]

The oldest Israelite literature about the Exodus from Egypt and the conquest of Canaan, the Song of the Sea in Exodus 15, describes Israel's entry into Canaan in the following terms:

> "The peoples heard, they trembled:
> Writhing seized the inhabitants of Philistia;
> Then, the chieftains of Edom were discomfited;
> The chiefs of Moab—terror seized them.
> All the inhabitants of Canaan melted away."
> Exodus 15:14-15[31]

The text places the Edomites and the Moabites in southern

Transjordan. It also locates the Philistines on the western side of the Jordan, no doubt on the southern Canaanite coast (cf. "the way of the Philistines" in Exodus 13:17 [E]). Yet the Philistines did not settle in Canaan until the early 12th century. The Philistines first appear in reliefs at the Egyptian temple at Medinet Habu, outside Luxor. Here, Ramesses III claims to have repulsed them, from Egyptian Asia, in his eighth year (c. 1192 B.C.E.). Further, no Philistine settlement has been archaeologically identified in Israel before about 1200 B.C.E. Though Exodus 15 no doubt retrojects later conditions back to the time of Israel's entry into Canaan, it reflects upon that development from no later than about 1100.

To date Israel's entry into Canaan much earlier than the late 13th century raises this question: Why does Israelite tradition[32]—even in its earliest stages—have no recollection whatever of the Philistines arrival in Canaan long *after* Israel was ensconced there (cf. Amos 9:7)? This problem is attenuated if Israel's arrival and that of the Philistines were virtually contemporary; it took time for the early Israelite settlement in the central hill country to spread to the regions bordering the Philistine coast (in fact, areas of Judah abutting Philistia were probably not settled until the 11th century).

This brings us to the crux of the matter, which is the relationship of the Exodus to the conquest. Bill Dever has devoted an entire talk to that subject, while I must restrict the articulation of my own view to a thumbnail sketch in this context. Still, in the 13th century, as just noted, a series of peoples emerge along the King's Highway* in Transjordan. Edom and Moab are mentioned in Egyptian documents. So are the Shasu, or pastoralists. The Bible recollects the existence of a Midianite league, and of Amalek, at about this time.** The people of Ammon, too, must have been in formation. Not very long afterward, Aramean kingdoms begin to arise in Syria, and Arameans are attested in northern Syria at the same time (with antecedents stretching back to the reign of Shalmaneser I [1274-

---

* The King's Highway (Numbers 20:17, 21:22) was the road running south from Damascus through Transjordan, and affording access to the central hill country through ancient roads at the Adama ford of the Jordan River and up the Wadi Far'a. From Damascus, caravan trade could be conducted with the hydraulic civilizations of the Euphrates and Tigris.
** Amalek: Exodus 17:8-16 (J); Numbers 13:29 (J), 24:20; Deuteronomy 25:17-19; Judges 6:3,33, 7:12; down to 2 Samuel 8:12 (cf. 1 Samuel 15). Midian: Exodus 2:15f, 3:1, 4:19, 18:1; Numbers 22:4,7 (all JE); Numbers 25, 31 (P); down to Judges 6-8.

1245 B.C.E.]). To these peoples—the Ammonites, the Moabites and especially the Arameans and the Edomites—the Israelites felt a close kinship. And the first Israelite settlements in the hills of Canaan probably stem from the latter part of the 13th century, too. These share their material culture with that of the Transjordanian populations, including not just pottery traditions and family organization, but also glyptic and naming traditions.[33]

The inference I draw is that a new population spread down from Syria along the King's Highway over the course of the 13th century. This is the population the Bible identifies as Hebrew, an ethnicon, it will be recalled, that is used in the Bible only when foreigners are referring to Israelites. At least at the end of the Iron Age, the Bible portrays the Hebrews as the rightful successors of an indigenous population of Canaanites, Amorites or Rephaim.[34]

What could have impelled the new population to settle among the non-Hebrews in Transjordanian and Cisjordanian Canaan? The 13th century was a period of extreme turmoil in northern Syria and the Balih basin—the plain of Aram in south-central Turkey and northern Syria—to which Israelite folklore traces Israel's roots.* In that century, Assyria gradually dismantled the indigenous Mitannian states and turned them into provinces. A considerable element of West Semitic speakers lived in the region north of the Euphrates along the Balih and Habur rivers. Some of them were pastoralists or dimorphic agrarians** in background, associated with hill territory and later referred to as Arameans.[35] No doubt many converted their assets into livestock and migrated away from heavy taxation.

Some of the migrants found their way not just into southern Syria and Transjordan, but into the central hills of Cisjordan.[36] Merneptah mentions this group in the celebrated Israel Stele.† Some of the evidence from the material culture suggests that the early Israelites enjoyed some familiarity with Canaanite culture.[37] Still,

---

* Abram came from Harran in JP (Genesis 11:31f., 12:4f.). The return to Aram to get wives for the children is referred to in Genesis 24; 28:10 (= Hosea 12:13) and Genesis 29-32. The tradition that an "Aramean was my father" is found in Deuteronomy 26:5. The whole notion of J and P's ethnology (Genesis 10-11), according to which the Arameans are close relations with the Israelites, also reflects this basic understanding.
** They spread the economic risk through a mixture of husbandry and extensive agriculture and horticulture.
† See Frank J. Yurco, "3,200-Year-Old Picture of Israelites Found in Egypt," *Biblical Archaeology Review*, September/October 1990.

most of the evidence linking the collared-rim jar, for example, to Canaanite towns, is susceptible to explanation on the basis of trade. Continuity in the pottery tradition between the Hebrew elements—including those in Transjordan—is susceptible to the same explanation if we adopt a model of gradual homesteading from Syria rather than of unified invasion. From differences in social organization—and its architectural articulations, from differences in household economy and from differences in economic strategies, I would conclude that Israelites, and their Transjordanian counterparts in Ammon, Moab and Edom, and farther north in Aram, were *not* indigenous to Canaan, and that their background lay in a combination of agriculture and husbandry, in many cases in a mountainous environment.

But it is inconceivable that all these new elements, who shared a common culture, should have participated in an Exodus from Egypt. The Arameans, Ammonites, Moabites and Edomites, at any rate, are not understood by the Israelites to have shared the Exodus experience: This indicates that they had no such national myth. And this, in turn, leaves us with the question whether earliest Israel in Canaan was itself the product of the Exodus, or whether, like the Jamestown colony in the United States, it was the beneficiary of a national myth formed from a subsequent experience.

Specifically, to understand the relationship of the Exodus to the conquest, we must ask, just what was the nature of the Exodus? As we have seen, much of the Exodus story is typologically true. That is, the narratives do not allow us to ascertain exactly to which people these events occurred, do not permit us even to claim that all the events occurred to a single group, but the details conform to the Canaanite experience of Late Bronze Egypt. There were Semites there, there was forced labor, there was brickmaking, there was intense building activity under Ramesses II, including of the city of Ramses. The list could easily be extended—Moses' name is clearly Egyptian,* the story of Moses growing up in the court mirrors the practice of Egyptian kings raising the children of their Semitic vassals as hos-

---

* As has long been recognized, "Moses" is the short form of a name like Ramesses or Thutmosis, which mean "Ra has begotten," "Thoth has begotten" or the like. The name means, "has begotten." The divine name originally attached to the verb has not survived. Or is the literary implication of the name that Moses himself begat the nation, Israel?

tages in the court. But it is most unlikely that a group of some three million people—or even 80,000, which is Manetho's figure—left Egypt down the Wadi Tumilat in the reign of Ramesses or Merneptah. It is completely unthinkable that any group of any related size went rattling around in the Sinai Peninsula or the Negev for any length of time thereafter.

Last year, at the Wild Animal Park in Escondido, California, my younger daughter got her first glimpse of a unicorn. She saw it unmistakably, until the oryx she was looking at turned its head, revealing that, in fact, it had two horns. And in that moment, she learned that the difference between the mundane and the magical is a matter of perspective. That is probably the case with the Exodus.

What if it is the case that the very Exodus is itself typologically true? We have reports of runaway slaves escaping down the Wadi Tumilat. An official pursuing two runaway slaves in the late 13th century arrived a day after leaving the capital, Ramses, at "the enclosure-wall of Tjeku"—the station at the end of the Wadi Tumilat in Exodus; the two slaves then continued by a southern route into the eastern desert.[38] The enclosure wall of Tjeku reflects Egyptian interest in controlling border traffic there—incoming and outgoing. Escapees from Egypt evidently might avail themselves of this route.

What *is* historically imaginable is repeated incidents of this stripe. We might even envision an instance in which a small group of pastoralists, tending sheep in the Wadi Tumilat, migrated out of Egypt, legally or illegally, in order to evade corvée. Such pastoralists, with no tradition of state labor, would regard Egyptian forms of taxation as nothing less than slavery. Yet, after a sufficient time in Egypt, they would also have assimilated some of the history of the Delta—and may even have identified themselves with the viceroy of a Hyksos king named Jacob. Of their own illustrious ancestry they had no doubt.

Escaping into the desert, too, was a sign that they had been touched by a god, and it is no coincidence that somewhere in the regions through which they migrated there was a "land of the Shasu (or, pastoralists) of *YHWH*," attested in Egyptian texts of the 14th or 13th century.[39] Nor, for that matter, is it in any way coincidental that it is from the same regions—Seir, the field of Edom—that Israelite liturgists of the Iron I period thought *YHWH* had come to conquer

Canaan (Judges 5:4; Exodus 15:15; Deuteronomy 33:2-3,29; Psalm 68:8-9,18; later, Habakkuk 3:3 and 1 Kings 19). The very modest beginnings of a cult of *YHWH* associated with an exodus from Egypt can thus be divined in some incident, or series of incidents, that would be invisible to us archaeologically and historically—as the Exodus is.

So far we have a cult located somewhere in the southern steppe of Canaan and related to an exodus from Egypt. Were this the end of the development, it is safe to say that the Exodus would have left no imprint whatever on what the poet calls "the sands of time." But it was not the end. For, somehow, the Exodus myth, and the community responsible for preserving it—and here, we should think in terms of a number of years, not of decades—came into contact with elements that were homesteading down the King's Highway in Transjordan.

The mechanics of this step are impossible to stipulate, and here we are essentially doomed to remain forever in the dark. What we *know* is that the group responsible for introducing the Exodus story into the culture of Cisjordanian immigrants from Syria (whom we may call the Israelites) found a compatible culture in these immigrants, a culture that was receptive to the notion that the Israelites were immigrants in the land, whose property had been converted into livestock in the 13th and 12th centuries. The affinity was in no way coincidental: The Israelites (the migrants from Syria and those with whom they established *connubium* in the central hills) felt this affinity for Edomites in general[40] (and for the nomadic Kenites[41]), and their folklore identified Esau, the ancestor of Edom, as the full brother of Jacob/Israel (Genesis 25:21-34; Deuteronomy 23:8; Hosea 12:4; Jeremiah 9:3; Amos 1:11).

The Exodus group found something else in the Israelites. Inside Cisjordan, the Israelites were the group most proximate to the centers of Egyptian control of Canaan. Of the "Hebrews"—Aramean, Ammonite, Moabite, Edomite, Arabian—they were most extensively exposed to sales of children into Egypt during times of famine, to Egyptian imposts, to Egyptian arms parading through the inland valleys and coastal roads of Cisjordan. Small wonder that they were also the most receptive to a cult myth conditioned on the assumption of escaping bondage to the Egyptians. It is impossible to say, now, whether the drowning of an Egyptian army in the Reed [Red] Sea celebrated in Exodus 15 occurred during the escape of the Exodus group from Egypt. The motif may be drawn from the drowning of a Canaanite army in the Jezreel Valley, related in Judges 5, or it may reflect some other event in which Israelites were implicated. In either case, the idea of defeating or escaping Egyptian arms is central.

The other factor in the development of the Exodus story is more central. For, in its Israelite incarnation, the Exodus story is also a promise of the land. Like the Mayflower Compact, it legitimated the ownership of the land, and, as in the case of the Pilgrims, the Israelites ratified the legitimation by eating the totem of the land, in their case a lamb rather than a turkey. The Exodus, without the conquest, would never have survived as a story.

From all this, it should be clear that we cannot know the precise relationship of the Exodus to the Israelite settlement in Canaan. What we *do* know is that the Exodus was certainly central to the ideology of the Israelites in Canaan already in Iron I. The victory at the sea in Exodus 15,[42] the tradition that *YHWH* marched forth from Edom to conquer Canaan,[43] the Egyptian reference to the land of the Shasu of *YHWH*[44] all point to the same conclusion. Sometime, relatively early in Iron I, Israel began to subscribe to a national myth of escape from Egypt, mediated by a god residing in the south (and outside Canaan), with the purpose of establishing a nation in Canaan. That national myth—justifying the Israelite land claims in Canaan— became a call to arms, a doctrine of Manifest Destiny, for a people newly arrived from the north and east.

The advent of Yahwism was a call to xenophobia against the lowland Canaanites, who are identified as the oppressor—a cultural stereotype that appears time and again in the earliest Israelite literature (Judges 5; Exodus 15, etc.). This xenophobia reflects antagonism on an ethnic level toward anyone whose ancestors had not participated in the Exodus. That is, the xenophobia of these texts is directed toward non-Israelites, inhabitants of the lowlands, Canaanites.

This, too, is the natural function of a national myth: such myths exclude others—as circumcision and as dietary restrictions do. The key thing to understand, however, is that in setting up a cult focused on liberation from slavery and on national enfranchisement in a land, ancient Israel was erecting a paradigm—not just excluding Canaanites—for the basic conditions under which an ethnic community could enjoy a sense both of separateness and of independence.

ENDNOTES

1. See generally J. Vansina, *Oral Tradition as History* (Madison: Univ. of Wisconsin Press, 1985), pp. 57-59.

2. Michael Walzer, *Exodus and Revolution* (New York: Basic, 1985).

3. See Ronald S. Hendel, "Sacrifice as a Cultural System: The Ritual Symbolism of Exodus 24, 3-8," *Zeitschrift für die alttestamentliche Wissenschaft* 101 (1989), pp. 366-390.

4. JE, for example has only eight plagues (Exodus 7:14-18, 20b-21a [blood]; 7:25-29, 8:1-11a [frogs]; 8:16-28 [flies]; 9:1-7 [pestilence among the livestock]; 9:13-29 [hail]; 10:1-19 [locusts]; 10:21-26 [darkness]; and 11:1-9, 12:21-27,29-36 [death of firstborn]). J alone would have had fewer plagues still, as pestilence (*dbr*) and hail (*brd*) form a doublet, the latter affecting cattle supposedly killed by the former. The number grew to ten in the present text.

5. The principle that in times of famine one sold one's children into slavery, and found grain in Egypt, is a telling one: Egyptian agriculture, after all, depended on the Nile flood rather than on the rainfall of western Asia. In one case of disastrous famine, related to the fall of the Hittite state in Anatolia and the collapse of urban Canaanite civilization at the end of the Late Bronze Age, Egypt alone was able to offer relief; see G.A. Wainwright, "Merneptah's Aid to the Hittites," *Journal of Egyptian Archaeology* 46 (1960), pp. 24ff.; M.C. Astour, "New Evidence on the Last Days of Ugarit," *American Journal of Archaeology* 69 (1965), pp. 253-258, on King Ammurapi of Ugarit forwarding Egyptian grain to Hatti.

A bit later, there is also evidence of shepherds entering Egypt in the vicinity of Goshen in order to graze their flocks. Under Seti II (1222-1216 B.C.E., high chronology), a frontier official related his readiness to admit the "nomadic tribes of Edom to the water holes of Per-Atum [biblical Pithom] of Merneptah Hotep-har-Maat of Tjeku, to sustain them and their [small?] cattle."—Papyrus Anastasi 6.51-61, late 13th century; see "Egyptian Historical Texts," transl. John A. Wilson, in *Ancient Near Eastern Texts Relating to the Old Testament* (*ANET*), 3rd ed., ed. James Pritchard (Princeton, NJ: Princeton Univ. Press, 1969), p. 259; James H. Breasted, *Ancient Records of Egypt* (*ARE*), 7 vols. (1906; reprinted) 3.368. (An earlier case, indicating that the practice was typical, is found in Breasted, *ARE* 3.10-12.) The continuation of this text shows that the commerce was a regular feature of the Bronze Age.

6. For the present purposes, anachronisms are unimportant, merely a sign that the narratives were codified far later than the initial recollection of the relevant events—for example, the fact that the Egyptian king is referred to as the pharaoh ("big house," a term first attested midway through the XVIIIth Dynasty), the alleged reliance of the patriarchs on camels, first domesticated outside Arabia in the 13th or 12th century, and the like, including toponyms. For Semites in power in Ramesside times, see S. Sauneron and J. Yoyotte, "Traces d'établissements asiatiques en Moyenne Egypte sous Ramsés II," *Revue d'Egyptologie* 7 (1951), pp. 67-70; A. Rowe, "Stelae of the Semite Ben-Azen" *Annales du Service des Antiquitiés de l'Egypt* 40 (1940), pp. 45-46. Note J. Vergote, *Joseph en Egypte* (Louvain: Publications Universitaires, 1959), pp. 203ff., for a Ramesside background to the Joseph story; Roland de Vaux, *Early History of Israel* (Philadelphia: Westminster, 1975), pp. 300ff. At the end of the XIXth Dynasty, Ramesses III reports (Wilson, "Egyptian Historical Texts," *ANET*, p. 260) there was also a Canaanite (Horite) usurper on the throne.

7. *ḥq3 ḥswt*, or "rulers of foreign lands."

8. The war against the Hyksos was first successfully prosecuted by the pharaoh Kamose, who recovered the territory from Thebes up to the Faiyum. See Wilson, "Egyptian Historical Texts," *ANET*, for the Carnarvon tablet and Karnak stele, p. 232f.; for the new stele, probably a continuation of the former, p. 554f. For further texts, see Donald B. Redford, *History and Chronology of the Eighteenth Dynasty of Egypt* (Toronto: Univ. of Toronto Press, 1967), p. 36.

9. Under the Hyksos, Hatshepsut recalled later in the early 15th century B.C.E. in her

Speos Artemidos inscription, temples and monuments went to ruin; the Hyksos ruled "without Re" (the Egyptian sun-god).

10. The rate of taxation was 20 percent: Genesis 41:34-36,48-49; cf. Vergote, *Joseph en Egypt*, pp. 190-192.

11. One verse relates that "Joseph was shepherding (with) his brothers among the sheep" (Genesis 37:2 [J]: *rô'eh 'et 'eḥāw* can mean either "he was shepherding his brothers" or "he was shepherding with his brothers." The ambiguity is deliberate: he shepherds sheep, but, as a shepherd, is also destined to be a ruler; he is destined to shepherd his brothers: Donald B. Redford, *A Study of the Biblical Story of Joseph (Genesis 37-50)*, Vetus Testamentum suppl. (Leiden: Brill, 1970), pp. 15-16.

12. See below, and Genesis 46:29. In Genesis 46:28, the Septuagint (LXX) identifies Goshen as Heroonpolis, identified in late sources as Tell Maskhuta. In Genesis 46:34, 45:10, LXX places it in Arabias, the 20th nome of Lower Egypt, whose capital was located at Faqus. John Van Seters (*The Hyksos* [New Haven, CT: Yale Univ. Press, 1965] p. 148) correspondingly locates Goshen in the region between the Pelusiac branch of the Nile and the Wadi Tumilat. H. Cazelles (*Autour de l'Exode* [Paris: Gabalda, 1987], pp. 233-239) argues a location outside Egypt, placing the Goshen of Joshua 11:16 in the zone between Kadesh-Barnea and Gaza, between Judah and Egypt. This approach lays too much stress on the putative implication that any "land of Goshen" must be outside Egypt (against Genesis 45:10,20, 47:11,27). Interestingly, the Bohairic, a Coptic text, relates Goshen in Genesis 46:28-29 to Pithom. Pithom has been identified with some confidence as Tell Maskhuta, on the Wadi Tumilat (below). In all, the location of Goshen on the eastern Wadi Tumilat and to the north of it seems to claim the balance of probability. But see Gerhard von Rad, *Genesis*, Old Testament Library (Philadelphia: Westminster, 1961), p. 394f.; Vergote, *Joseph en Egypte*, pp. 183-186.

13. "Close by me, you and your sons and your sheep and your cattle and all that is yours" (Genesis 45:10 [J]).

14. E? Cf. Richard E. Friedman, *Who Wrote the Bible?* (New York: Summit, 1987).

15. Especially instructive is the exchange when Joseph brings his family into the pharaoh's presence (Genesis 46:31-47:11 [J]). Joseph instructs his brothers to say, "'Your servants have been herders from our youth until now, both we and our fathers,' so that you may settle in the land of Goshen, for all shepherds are an abomination to Egypt." In contrast to the earlier explanation of the narrator that the Egyptians abominated all "Hebrews" (Genesis 43:32 [J]), the significance of the identification of shepherds as an abomination to Egyptians is unmistakable: the reference is to the Hyksos, and Joseph's strategy involves an expression of solidarity with the Hyksos: E.A. Speiser, *Genesis*, Anchor Bible 1 (Garden City, N.Y.: Doubleday, 1960), p. 345.

Consider that, in the storyteller's imagination, the purpose of the Israelites' declaring themselves shepherds to the pharaoh is to secure a land grant in Goshen, "close by" the capital in which Joseph and the pharaoh rule. To announce that the brothers, and, indeed, Joseph himself, are things abominable to the pharaoh does not, however, seem a strategy devised to elicit an award of "the best part of the land," where the pharaoh's own herds are pastured (Genesis 47:6). The text thus presupposes that the Israelites are making the declaration to a pharaoh who, like themselves, is not at home with native Egyptians—a Hyksos king, to be precise.

16. The Hyksos capital, Avaris, was first occupied in the 18th century B.C.E.: the lowest stratum (G) produced a radiocarbon dating of 1870-1720 B.C.E.

17. Manfred Bietak, *Avaris and Piramesse* (Oxford: Oxford Univ. Press, 1981), pp. 236-237, 271. There was a break in occupation, however, apparently from LB I to the last part of LB IIA.

18. Bietak, *Avaris and Piramesse*, pp. 278-279. It was silting in the Pelusiac branch of the Nile that forced the kings of the XXIst Dynasty to remove the capital from Avaris/Ramses.

19. The Four-Hundred-Year Stele records the appropriation of the Seth cult by Ramesses II, whose image and titulary are attached to it, see Breasted, *ARE* 3.539-540. An enormous XVIIIth Dynasty temple, surrounded by large numbers of trees (a grove to Asherah?) persisted into the XXIst Dynasty and may be identified as the temple of Seth (Bietak, *Avaris and Piramesse*, pp. 269-271, 282). But cf. Breasted, *ARE* 4.362, indicating that Ramesses III constructed a temple to Seth there. On the popularity of the Canaanite goddess Astarte in LB

Egypt, see Wilson, "Egyptian Historical Texts," *ANET*, p. 250 (a).

20. See Aharon Kempinski, "Jacob in History," *Biblical Archaeology Review*, Jan./Feb. 1988, pp. 42ff. *Y'qb-HR*, possibly Jacob-'el or, less probably, Jacob-haddu ("'El/Haddu will/ should protect/prosecute [enemies]"). Kempinski has argued, on the basis of finds in tombs from Tel Cabri on the northern coast of Israel, that Jacob was in origin a Canaanite dynastic name of the 18th century B.C.E., later adopted by the Hyksos dynasty, see "Some Observations on the Hyksos (XVth) Dynasty and Its Canaanite Origins," in *Pharaonic Egypt. The Bible and Christianity*, ed. S. Israelit-Groll (Jerusalem: Magnes, 1985), pp. 129-137. More recently see "Two Scarabs of Yakabum," in *Studies in Egyptology presented to Miriam Lichtheim*, ed. S. Israelit-Groll (Jerusalem: Magnes, 1990), pp. 632-634. There is the possibility, however, that the Hyksos Jacob was a nomarch during the early stages of penetration of the Delta in the late Middle Kingdom and that the seal at Cabri derives from relations there with his dynasty.

21. See P. Kyle McCarter, Jr. "The Patriarchal Age," in *Ancient Israel*, ed. Hershel Shanks (Englewood Cliffs, NJ: Prentice-Hall; Washington, DC: Biblical Archaeology Society, 1988), p. 8, and a forthcoming treatment in Halpern, *A History of Israel in Her Land*, Anchor Bible Reference Library (Garden City, NY: Doubleday).

22. See R.A. Caminos, *Late-Egyptian Miscellanies* (London: Oxford Univ. Press, 1954), p. 491; J. Bottéro, *Le problème des Habiru*, Cahiers de la Société Asiatique 12 (Paris: Imprimerie Nationale, 1954), p. 187f. The texts (Papyrus Leiden 348, vs. 6:6; 349, r. 15) concern grain rations for the soldiers and 'Apiru transporting stone for "the great pylon" of a building of Ramesses II in Memphis. The term 'Apiru first appears in texts of the Middle Kingdom and continues in use into the XXth Dynasty.

23. See Caminos, *Late-Egyptian Miscellanies*, p. 188. The laborers in the biblical account are deprived of their straw allotment and compelled to gather straw locally in order to meet their quotas (Exodus 5:5-19). That is, the nature of Israel's conscription is lavishly illustrated by Egyptian documents and art: corvée among Semites, brickmaking with straw, even brickmaking quotas are amply documented. See esp. C.F. Nims, "Bricks without Straw," *Biblical Archaeologist* 13 (1950), pp. 22-28. For the scale of such enterprises, note the XIXth Dynasty scroll assigning "stablemasters"—presumably officers like the Israelite overseers in Exodus 5—quotas amounting in all to 80,000 bricks. See on this and further, Kenneth H. Kitchen, "From the Brickfields of Egypt," *Tyndale Bulletin* 27 (1976), pp. 136-147; A. Spenser, *Brick Architecture in Ancient Egypt* (Warminster, UK: Aris and Phillips, 1979).

24. To the Israelite request, for example, for permission to desist from work and celebrate a festival for *YHWH*, "the god of the Hebrews" (Exodus 3:18, 5:3, 8:23), scholars compare the respite accorded to corvée laborers on days of special sacrifices. See Kitchen, *Ancient Orient and Old Testament* (Downers Grove, IL: Intervarsity, 1975), pp. 156-157; Nahum M. Sarna, "Israel in Egypt," in Shanks, *Ancient Israel*, p. 41.

25. See Kitchen, *The Bible in Its World* (Exeter, UK: Paternoster, 1977), pp. 76-77. The kings of the XIXth Dynasty generally restricted their major public works to the southern Delta; even their northern residence in Memphis was south of the Delta. The last king of the dynasty, Horemheb (1347-c. 1318 on the high chronology), was the first to undertake a project at Avaris. Seti I (c. 1316-1304 B.C.E.) installed a palace at Avaris/Per-Ramses. But his son, Ramesses II, transferred the capital to this site.

26. Amenhotep III, in a stele to Amun later defaced by Akhenaten, speaks of settlements of Canaanites (Hurru) surrounding his temple to Amun west of Thebes, see Breasted, *ARE* 2.884. This is the stone, restored by Seti I, on the back of which Merneptah inscribed the Israel Stele.

27. In Memphis alone there was a merchant "camp of the Tyrians" and temples to the Canaanite god Baal and to Baal and Ashtarte. Canaanite goddesses, Anat and Qudshu, entered the Egyptian pantheon during the XVIIIth Dynasty, and the cult of the god Reshep flourished in the Delta. One father even accuses a son who has reached the Delta of adopting Asiatic practices. See generally Donald B. Redford, *Akhenaten, the Heretic King* (Princeton, NJ: Princeton Univ. Press, 1984), pp. 27-29; R. Stadelmann, *Syrisch-palästinensische Gottheiten in Agypten* (Leiden: Brill, 1967), cited there.

28. On Semitic slaves, see G. Posener, "Une liste de noms propres étrangers" *Syria* 18 (1937), pp. 183-197; see also W. Helck, *Der Einfluss der Militär-führer in der 18. ägyptischen Dynastie* (Hildesheim, Germ.: Olms, 1964), p. 21.

29. See endnote 17 on the location of Ramses at Tell ed-Dab'a, and John van Seters, *The Hyksos: A New Investigation* (New Haven, CT: Yale Univ. Press, 1966), pp. 127-151; see esp. Manfred Bietak, *Tell el-Dab'a II. Der Fundort im Rahmen einer archäologisch-geographischen Untersuchung über das ägyptische Ostdelta* (Vienna: Oesterreichische Akademie der Wissenschaften, 1975), pp. 179-221. The identification of Tanis (San) with Avaris/Ramses, long held to be most probable, is precluded by the absence from that site of any Asiatic material culture antedating the 11th century. Interestingly, the onomasticon of Amenope, at the end of the Ramesside era, still reflects the knowledge that Tanis and Per-Ramses were distinct sites, see Alan H. Gardiner, *Ancient Egyptian Onomastica* II (London: Oxford Univ. Press, 1947), #410 and #417.

On the location of Pithom, for Merneptah's building activity there, see Papyrus Anastasi 6.51-61, translated in Breasted, *ARE* 3.638. In Wilson, "Egyptian Historical Texts," *ANET*, p. 259, a border official reports the passage of "pastoralists of Edom (*'dwm*)" from the fort of Merneptah—in the region of Tjeku, (*Tkw*)—to the pools of "Per-'Atum of Merneptah" (or Pithom). This indication of settlement—and use of the pools by Edomite elements for grazing—in New Kingdom times precludes an identification of Merneptah's Per-'Atum with Tell el-Maskhuta: Maskhuta was unoccupied from the time of the Middle Kingdom until the Saite period. See John S. Holladay, *Cities of the Delta, Part III/Tell el-Maskhutah,* American Research Center in Egypt Reports 6 (Malibu, CA: Undena, 1982), pp. 6, 19; Redford, "Exodus I, 11," *Vetus Testamentum (VT)* 13 (1963), pp. 401-418. Contrast W. Helck, "Tjeku und die Ramses-Stadt," *VT* 15 (1965), pp. 35-48, for an effort to locate Pithom at Tell el-Maskhuta and to identify it with Tjeku—an effort that must be judged abortive in light both of the archaeological evidence and of the clear indications from Papyrus Anastasi 6 that Tjeku was a region.

The other principal candidate in the Wadi Tumilat, Tell er-Retaba, halfway (eight and a half miles) between Maskhuta and the Delta, remains a possibility. A Roman milestone found at Maskhuta seems to indicate that Tell er-Retaba is that site (Alan H. Gardiner, "The Delta Residence of the Ramessides," *Journal of Egyptian Archaeology* 5 [1918], pp. 127-138, 179-200, 242-271, esp. p. 269; recently, William H. Stiebing, Jr., *Out of the Desert? Archaeology and the Exodus/Conquest Narratives* [Buffalo, NY: Prometheus, 1989], p. 58). Holladay's survey did not detect occupation at Tell er-Retaba before the XXth Dynasty either, but there were signs of settlement shortly thereafter, and the possibility of a small New Kingdom establishment therefore remains (see Holladay, *Tell el-Maskhutah* 6 and in conversation). However, this may have no direct bearing on the location of the more ancient site.

In any event, Pithom was located in the region of Tjeku, on the eastern border of Egypt, where nomads might enter from Asia. Tjeku was probably biblical Succoth—Egyptian *t* corresponding to Hebrew *s*—identified in late texts as Israel's first stopping place after its departure from the city, Ramses (Exodus 13:20; Numbers 33:5-6); the Hebrew term may well reflect a familiarity with the Egyptian terminology—indicating in what area the Israelites encamped (other references to waystations include areas such as the wilderness of Sin, the Reed Sea and the like), rather than giving a name to a particular encampment.

Probably identifying Ramses as Tanis, the author of one Pentateuchal source (probably E) felt called upon to explain the route of the Exodus from Egypt: "When pharaoh sent the people forth, God did not lead them by the way of the land of the Philistines [i.e., the coastal route]. God diverted the people onto the way of the wilderness of the Reed Sea . . . " (Exodus 13:17-18). This can only mean that instead of taking the direct route eastward from Tanis, between Lake Menzaleh and Lake Ballah, by Qantara and past the fortress of Sile, the Israelites were deflected southward, to the region of the Wadi Tumilat, between Lake Ballah and Lake Timsah to the south.

The Wadi Tumilat is also the area most probably to be identified as the biblical Goshen, where the Israelites take up residence. It was "the best of the land of Egypt" (Genesis 45:10, 47:6,11) where one could eat "the fat of the land"—agricultural produce, including cucumbers, melons, leeks, onions and garlic (Numbers 11:5)—and sustain extensive herds (as Genesis 45:10, 46:34, 47:3-4; Exodus 12:38), both of caprovines and of draft animals. Indeed, even the pharaoh's flocks were pastured there (Genesis 47:6). Conditions in the Wadi Tumilat area, which is not so marshy as the lower Delta, evince all these traits. The traditional identification of Goshen with the Wadi Tumilat, in fact, certainly dates to the time when the name of Pithom (Tell el-Maskhuta) was added to the text of Exodus 1:11, which is to say, at least to the sixth century B.C.E. See John S. Holladay, "'And they built for Pharaoh Store-cities, Pithom and Ramses (Exodus 1:11c).' An Archaeological Whodunnit," *Canadian Mediterranean Institute Bulletin* (Summer 1987).

The introduction of Pithom into Exodus 1:11 is explicable if refugees from Judah, who settled there in the Saite era, encountered the Semitic Middle Bronze pottery on the site from the Hyksos era or, as Holladay suggests, learned of earlier Semitic occupation from local informants. Yet the identification of the site as one built earlier by Israelites presupposes Israel's earlier residence in the Wadi Tumilat. In other words, the tradition that Israel inhabited Goshen is older than the introduction of Pithom into the Exodus account; this is why Pithom, of all the towns in which Judahites later settled, is singled out as a city of the oppression.

On the location of Goshen in the Wadi Tumilat, see esp. M. Har-El, *The Sinai Journeys* (San Diego, CA: Ridgefield, 1983), pp. 301-307. An alternate route for the Exodus, possibly along the coast in the line from Herakleopolis to Pelusium, or farther south in the region of Daphnae, is not to be excluded—either at some earlier stage of Israelite tradition or in terms of the historical Exodus. See generally, Yohanan Aharoni, *The Land of the Bible. A Historical Geography*, 2nd ed. (Philadelphia: Westminster, 1979), pp. 195-200.

The term "Goshen" (like the term "Tjeku") probably designates not just the Wadi Tumilat but a region stretching from the Wadi Tumilat toward the Pelusiac branch of the Nile (van Seters, *Hyksos*, p. 148). Goshen was "in the land of Ramses" (Genesis 47:11 [J]), which is to say, in the hinterland of the capital. Moreover, the assumption of the Genesis and Exodus narratives is that Israel dwelled in the vicinity of the city Ramses. Not only does the Exodus begin from Ramses (Numbers 33:3,5; Exodus 12:37), but Moses and Aaron repeatedly address both the pharaoh and the Israelites, and no narrator suggests that this mediation involved significant travel. Similarly, the daughter of the pharaoh is said to have found the infant Moses in the reeds of the Nile's bank in the presence of Moses' sister, who recommended his mother as a nursemaid (Exodus 2:3-9)—J's text, thus, situates the household at Ramses. Possibly, the earliest traditions placing Israel in Goshen presupposed that the city Ramses was at Tell ed-Dab'a on the Pelusiac branch of the Nile, rather than at Tanis to the north. Yet this must remain unsure: The tradition has adjusted to the transfer of the capital, making the assumption that the capital at Tanis was adjacent to Goshen. Thus, the possibility exists that the Israelite authors located Goshen between the Pelusiac and the Tanitic arms of the Nile (and, thus, the flight by way of Succoth to the south of Goshen). Indeed, Egyptians today identify the Ibn-Ezra synagogue (that of the Cairo Genizah) as the place where the pharaoh's daughter found Moses on the Nile. As the capital city migrates, so does the residence of the ancient Israelites.

30. Generally, see R.G. Boling, *The Early Biblical Community in Transjordan*, Social World of Biblical Antiquity Series (Sheffield, UK: Almond, 1988). On Moab, see Wilson, "Egyptian Historical Texts," *ANET*, p. 243; on Edom, see above for Papyrus Anastasi 6.51-61 under Merneptah. The land of (the Shasu, i.e., pastoralists of) Seir ($\check{s}^3$-'-r-i-r^3), later known to Israel as Edomite territory, is mentioned in Ramesses II's Amara West hypostyle geographical list, and Ramesses III or Ramesses IV speaks of Seir as being controlled by Shasu pastoralists, whom he plundered and captured (Papyrus Harris 1.76:9), without identifying them as Edomite. A XXIst Dynasty literary text (Papyrus Pushkin 127,5:5) may suggest that a route to Mesopotamia ran through Seir ($\check{s}^3$-'^{3}-i-r^3), but the geography envisioned is not obvious (across northern Arabia?). The same is true of a reference to destruction of pastoralists in the hills of s-$\check{s}$-'-r-i (Seir?) on the east side of an obelisk of Ramesses II found at Tanis (P. Montet and G. Goyon, *Kêmi* 5 [1935-1937], pl. 3). El Amarna letters (EA) 288:25-27, from Abdi-Hepa, governor of Jerusalem under Amenhotep III and Akhenaten, can be rendered, loosely, "I am at war—as far as the lands of Se-e-ri, as far as the town of Gath-Karmel—all the governors are at peace, and I am at war." This text is also ambiguous, especially as to the identity of Gath-Karmel; however, whether this is identical with Judahite Carmel, with Gath-Karmel of EA 289:18-19 (to the north) or some other locus (as Philistine Gath), the passage can be construed to depict Seir as Abdi-Hepa's southernmost (or easternmost) horizon.

For El Amarna letters, see now *The Amarna Letters*, ed. William L. Moran (Baltimore, MD: Johns Hopkins Univ. Press, 1992). For editions of these texts concerning Edom, see M. Weippert, *Edom. Studien und Materialen zur Geschichte der Edomiter auf Grundschriftlicher und archäologischen Quellen*, Ph.D. dissertation (Tübingen, 1971), pp. 31-48. Ammon is not named in any record until Iron II, but was probably organized, as biblical accounts indicate (esp. Judges 10:6-12:6), in Iron I. On the appearance of Israel, and of the Arameans in Syria, in just this period, see below.

31. On the antiquity and interpretation of Exodus 15, see Frank M. Cross, *Canaanite Myth and Hebrew Epic* (Cambridge, MA: Harvard Univ. Press, 1973), pp. 112-144.

32. As, for example, Genesis 21:32,34, 26:1-18, which portray the Philistines as having been present in Canaan already in the patriarchal (i.e., Middle Bronze) era.

33. See M.M. Ibrahim, "The Collared-rim Jar of the Early Iron Age," in *Archaeology in the Levant*, ed. P.R. Moorey and P. Parr (Warminster, UK: Aris & Phillips, 1978), pp. 116-126; "Siegel und Siegelabdrucke aus Sahāb," *Zeitschrift des deutschen Palästina-Vereins* 99 (1983), pp. 43-53. For the naming traditions, Jeffrey H. Tigay, *You Shall Have No Other Gods*, Harvard Semitic Studies 31 (Atlanta: Scholars Press, 1986); as Professor Frank Cross long ago observed, in conversation, the theophoric elements in the onomastica of Ammon, Moab and Edom, insofar as it is known to us, seem to conform to Israelite practice in naming either the chief god or some more general epithet (El, Baal, etc.) that can be construed as pertaining to him.

34. Deuteronomy 2:5+12,9-11,19-21. In the Deuteronomic presentation the Philistines, "who went out from Caphtor (on Crete)," are part of the divinely ordered succession to the giant aborigines (cf. Amos 2:9)—Deuteronomy 2:23. The ethnology of this chapter is identical to that of Genesis 14.

35. See A.K. Grayson, *Assyrian Royal Inscriptions*, vol. 2 (Wiesbaden: Harrassowitz, 1976) 2.775, for the association of the Arameans (here, Ahlamu, later to be called Ahlamu-Arameans and Arameans) with hill country terrain. The first reference to Arameans proper comes under Tiglath-pileser I (1114-1076 B.C.E.).

36. For Transjordan, note B. MacDonald, *The Wadi el Ḥaṣa Archaeological Survey 1979-1983, West-Central Jordan* (Waterloo, Can: Wilfrid Laurier University, 1988), pp. 11, 168-189, with one LB site, 6 transitional LB-Iron sites and 33 Iron I sites, not counting the 13 sites listed as transitional from Iron I to Iron II or the 14 undifferentiated Iron Age sites. Further, P.E. McGovern, *The Late Bronze and Early Iron Ages of Central Transjordan: The Baqʿah Valley Project, 1977-1981* (Philadelphia: University Museum, Univ. of Pennsylvania, 1986), pp. 340-341; J.M. Miller, *Archaeological Survey of the Kerak Plateau* (Atlanta: Scholars Press, 1991), pp. 193-197; Israel Finkelstein, "Edom in the Iron I," forthcoming in *Levant*. For discussion of Iron I Moabite toponymy in dialogue with biblical place-names, see Miller, "The Israelite Journey through (around) Moab and Moabite Toponymy," *Journal of Biblical Literature* 108 (1989), pp. 577-595. For Cisjordan, see Finkelstein, *The Archaeology of the Israelite Settlement* (Jerusalem: Israel Exploration Society, 1988); "The Land of Ephraim Survey 1980-1987: Preliminary Report," *Tel Aviv* 15-16 (1988-1989), pp. 117-183; Adam Zertal, "The Israelite Settlement in the Hill Country of Manasseh," Ph.D. dissertation (Tel Aviv University, 1986).

37. See the talk by W.G. Dever.

38. Papyrus Anastasi 5.19:7-20:2, Wilson, "Egyptian Historical Texts," *ANET*, p. 259.

39. See Manfred Weippert, *The Settlement of the Israelite Tribes in Palestine* (London: SCM, 1971), pp. 105-106.

40. Genesis 25:21-34, 27, 32, 36 (JE); Deuteronomy 23:8.

41. Judges 1:16, 4:11,17, 5:24-27; 1 Samuel 15:6, 27:10, 30:29.

42. See Cross, *Canaanite Myth*, pp. 112-144.

43. Judges 5:4-5; Deuteronomy 33:2-3, 26-29; Exodus 15:4, 13-17; Psalm 68:18; Habakkuk 3:3.

44. See Weippert, *Settlement of the Israelite Tribes*.

Questions & Answers

There was a large volcanic eruption, in Thera, I believe, which caused huge tidal waves over the Delta. Apparently one could observe the fire over the entire Mediterranean area. Could you explain how this fits in with the myth that you mentioned?

There have been a number of theories about the Exodus predicated on the assumption that the events as they're described in the Book of Exodus occurred at the time of the Exodus. We don't have an exact date for the eruption of Thera. The latest revisionist hypothesis is 1620 B.C.E. or thereabouts. I've seen dates down into the 15th century B.C.E. People say that if the plume of the volcanic eruption at Thera rose 30 miles into the air, you would have been able to see it from the Egyptian Delta. This then becomes the pillar of fire and cloud of smoke that the Israelites followed—not exactly the right direction, but they followed it anyway. (Laughter.) Two things come out of this. It used to be that we associated the explosion of Thera with the decline or the complete eradication of Minoan culture. It is often connected with the myth of Atlantis. As the story was retold, over time Thera became the island that sank, rather than the island that exploded. I suspect that the Thera story is actually the origin of the Sodom and Gomorrah story in Israel. Basically the Atlantis myth and the Sodom and Gomorrah story are the same story, just set in different environments.

Is Thera the pillar of cloud in the Exodus story? Quite possibly. Can we tie the Exodus chronologically to the Thera explosion? No, there's no chance that we can do that.

When did the word "Transjordan" emerge as a geographical term? If Merneptah had gone 50 or 80 miles east and wanted to brag about the conquest of that land, would he have referred to it as Transjordan? Isn't "trans-" a Roman prefix?

It's a good question. What you're saying is that I should not take the Merneptah Stele to imply that the Israelites are in Cisjordan. Is that correct?

No, no my question is, when did the word "Transjordan" emerge as a geographical term?

Not as a concept, just as a geographical term?

Just as a geographical term.

Well you do get words in Hebrew like '*Ever ha-Yarden* already in the biblical period, "across the Jordan," which is what Transjordan means—and which is where the British stole it from, by the way.

I'd like to endorse the use of names as an indicator of the origin of these traditions (which is also very helpful in other fields like British history). I think you make a very good case for the patriarchal period coinciding with Middle Bronze and with the Hyksos. But when you apply this kind of thinking to the actual Exodus, you get a very different kind of answer. You said the name "Moses" is an Egyptian name. In fact, it's a made-up name. It's a made-up Egyptian name meaning "son of" without being son of anything. This may be an alarm bell that here we have a story which is made up in much the same way as that of Romulus, which is also definitely a made-up name. This corresponds with what is generally agreed on in early Roman history as being almost entirely fictitious. So one should not place the actual Exodus story on this kind of evidence. One should place it on a very different basis from the fairly solid picture of the earlier sojourn in Egypt coinciding with the time of the Hyksos.

There is something behind the Israelite tradition. The basic problem we all run up against—and this is true of the peasant revolt school or the conquest theory, and even the so-called archaeological approach to the conquest—the problem is that you wind up with Israel with an Exodus tradition, a tradition of having been in bondage in Egypt.

What about Americans having British ancestors or European ancestors. Is it an ancestor myth?

There's got to be something behind it. It doesn't have to be what it says it is, and it certainly wasn't all-encompassing.

But there is something behind it?

Exactly. As to Moses' name, by the way, we have names like "Bonnie," not Bonnie and Clyde, but just Bonnie, which we call hypocoristic, which is a fancy word for nickname. "Bonnie" is a short form of "So and so has given birth" or "So and so has created a child." It's exactly the same as Moses—only the god's name has been clipped off and a nickname has been made out of it. For example, if you took the name "Johnson" and just called the person "Son" that would be the equivalent of the name Moses.

I found some of what you said confusing. I'll try to clarify what I mean. Are you saying that the story of the Exodus was written years after it occurred by a group of people who tried to create a mythological, for lack of a better word, framework for explaining why Jews do certain things, such as circumcision and not eating pork, and for saying they [the Jews] are connected to the Exodus, to the Canaanite land: This is how we got here and this is how and why we are where we are?

Let me clarify.

And how many years were there between when the events occurred and when they were written?

Number one, the earliest date for the writing down of any of this material would be the tenth century B.C.E. I think that's an early date. I think that's early by a century or more for the J source. And I think that the other sources that speak to this issue—the old poetry in Exodus 15 and Judges 5 and Deuteronomy 33—are probably Iron I (1200-1000 B.C.E.). Regardless of which model you use to reconstruct the rise of Israel, there is a considerable period of time passing between the events you reconstruct and the writing down of these accounts. When the accounts were reduced to writing, they were fixed—more or less. Although new accounts kept being generated, and they differ from the old accounts. What this reflects is the process of retelling. Now you asked me whether a bunch of people got together and concocted this story. I don't think that's exactly what happened.

I didn't say concocted the story; I said wrote the story down.

O.K. So are you satisfied with that?

No. My question is—Are you saying that the Exodus story in the Bible is a story that was written down hundreds of years after the event to give identity, or a natural myth, explaining two things: (1) why Jews did certain cultural things like circumcision and dietary laws and (2) how they came in possession of this land.

What I'm saying is that the Passover, which became the celebration of the Exodus, had already become freighted with questions of that variety. And the Exodus myth developed in the context of the Paschal celebration into the form in which we have it now.

Is there any connection between the development of the Israelite God Yahweh, the one god, and Akhenaten's institution of the one sun-god?

Not in my view. We have another speaker, Kyle McCarter, who may choose to address that question more specifically.

I have read somewhere that there was recorded in Egyptian history an Exodus at some time.

We have fragments of Egyptian history by a man named Manetho who was an Egyptian priest, writing in Greek [in the third century B.C.E.]. These fragments are preserved in a number of classical sources, such as Josephus, Africanus and Eusebius. But Manetho seems to be relying secondhand on the biblical story in order to reconstruct the Exodus and to tell it in a way that is abusive of, and hostile to, the Israelites. So I don't regard that as an independent witness or as reliable testimony.

Introduction

*W*hat motivated the changes that previous speakers have
noted in the archaeological record when the Israelites emerged
in the central hill country of Canaan? What were the reasons
behind the emergence? Did religion play a part? Bill Dever
candidly admitted that archaeology couldn't provide an
answer to this question. So it's quite a challenge for our last
speaker to deal with the question of religion—the origin of the
Israelite religion and how religion affected this emerging
people, Israel. I don't think we could have gotten anyone better
in the entire world to explore this difficult aspect of our subject
today than Kyle McCarter. Kyle also received his Ph.D. from
Harvard. He is one of the broadest, most eclectic biblical
scholars I know. He can deal with so many different aspects of
the discipline—from archaeology to ancient languages to
inscriptions to the biblical text itself. He is the author of the
two-volume commentary on Samuel in the Anchor Bible
series. He is a past president of the American Schools of
Oriental Research. He presently holds the chair—I wonder
how he feels when he wakes up in the morning knowing the
title of his chair—the William Foxwell Albright chair at the
Johns Hopkins University. Albright was of course the doyen of
biblical archaeologists of an earlier generation. Kyle is the
William Foxwell Albright Professor of Biblical and Ancient
Near Eastern Studies. It's a pleasure to introduce to you my
friend Kyle McCarter.—H.S.

P. KYLE McCARTER, JR.

The Origins
of
Israelite Religion

I t's a special treat to share the podium with colleagues of the caliber that Hershel has gathered together for us. Bill Dever speaks with as much authority as anyone in the world on the subject of the archaeology of the region that we are interested in and Baruch Halpern has written the most important book to date on our subject. So it's an honor to be here with them and to hear what they've said. It has created a problem for me, though, because they've already said everything there is to say. (Laughter.) You've heard it all now, and I've decided to talk about the legend of Robin Hood. (Laughter.) Not really.

Hershel, I want to comment on an interesting fact, I believe I see a new consensus emerging. I think we've gotten far enough along on this subject where we can begin to say that there is a new commonality emerging among scholars about what occurred at the beginning of the Iron Age in Palestine Israel. I say this because I find myself so much in agreement with what Bill and Baruch have said.

And I sense the collapse of the paradigm that we set for ourselves in the past—a paradigm that Hershel articulated to you. We posited three models for the origin of the Israelite state—military conquest, peaceful settlement and social revolution—and asked which of these three was true.

That paradigm has become obsolete, and we are at the point where we don't have to talk about three possible models anymore. We are developing a new model.

I think the basis of the new model is Baruch Halpern's book on *The Emergence of Israel in Canaan*.[1] Working from the arguments in that book and other similar scholarship, we have begun to develop a new consensus. If you look back on the things that the three of us have said today, I expect you'll see more common features than disagreements. It's not because we all went to Harvard (laughter); the subject is too new for us to have been indoctrinated into any kind of conformity. There is no sense in which Bill, Baruch and I are part of a group of investigators who are trying to persuade our colleagues of a new way of looking at the complex phenomenon of the beginning of the Iron Age in Palestine.

At this point, however, I do want to introduce a note of disagreement, and I'll use it to introduce my remarks. I don't claim to be an archaeologist. I work with historical and literary materials. So let me begin by offering a literary objection to a common assertion made by archaeologists about the Book of Judges: the assertion that the account of the conquest of Canaan in Judges 1 is a more authentic picture of what went on in Iron I than is the larger account in the Book of Joshua. Judges 1 gives what seems to be a much more realistic, modest and measured account of the conquest.* In contrast to the swift and thorough capture of the land described in Joshua, Judges 1 says that most tribes didn't succeed fully in driving out the people in their assigned territories, though maybe one or two tribes did. Therefore, we are told, Judges 1 may be an earlier, less ideologically based and historically more reliable account than that of Joshua.

But let me mention a very interesting fact. If you examine one of the most important witnesses to the ancient text of the Hebrew

* Yigael Yadin, "Is the Biblical Account of the Israelite Conquest of Canaan Historically Reliable?" and Abraham Malamat, "How Inferior Israelite Forces Conquered Fortified Canaanite Cities," both in *Biblical Archaeology Review*, March/April 1982.

Bible, namely the Septuagint, the early Greek translation of the Hebrew Bible, you will find that in all likelihood in its earliest form it
lacked Judges 1 altogether. When you come to the end of the Book
of Joshua, you find yourself reading the story of Ehud, the first of the
great heroes of the Book of Judges. What that almost certainly means
is that the Hebrew text from which the translator of the earliest
Greek version of Joshua-Judges was working didn't have Judges 1 in it.

Now, this text-critical fact is open to more than one interpretation. On the surface, all it means is that in antiquity there was a text
of Judges that didn't have chapter 1 in it, and that chapter 1 was
added to that text later. It was inserted into the Greek by a later
Greek translator. What are the possible interpretations of this shorter
version of Judges? It's possible that someone removed Judges 1 from
a text of Joshua-Judges that included it. But that's not very likely.
Ancient scribes were inclined to be inclusive. They respected, even
revered the text they worked with. And so a basic principle that we
work with as textual critics is that the scribes are not likely to have
removed something. If you have two versions of a text—one longer
and one shorter—it's much more likely that the shorter text is earlier
and the longer text is later, that something was added along the way.
So it is very likely that there was a time when the Hebrew text of
Joshua-Judges existed without this chapter that is so crucial to the
archaeological discussion here. Or to put it differently, at some point
this chapter existed as an independent document and was inserted in
the Bible.

Even so, this fact could mean more than one thing. It could be
that Judges 1 was a very ancient document that was added at a very
late date to the biblical text. Alternatively, it could be that Judges 1
was simply a very late document. These possibilities have led me to
ask myself the question how Judges 1 might be understood as a late
document rather than a very early document? I had been taught the
theory that you heard from Hershel and Bill that Judges 1 was probably a more authentic and reliable account of the conquest than
Joshua and likely, therefore, to be quite ancient. But now I ask
myself if there is a way of thinking of Judges 1 as a late composition.

If you read Judges 1 very carefully you will find an interesting
thing. It doesn't say in every case that the tribes were unable to drive
out the local inhabitants from their allotted territories. It says that in

most cases, but there are two exceptions who were able to drive out the local inhabitants. One is the case of the tribe of Judah and the other is the tribe of Benjamin. Now the effect of saying this is to suggest that the most consistently Israelite population, the least mixed population, is in the tribal territories of Judah and Benjamin. If you consider this suggestion within the context of the history of Israel, and if you look at post-Exilic history in particular, you'll find a time when most of the land of Israel apart from Judah and Benjamin had been lost to the government in Jerusalem for an extended period of time. Moreover, the post-Exilic period is the time from which we have literature that touches on the reforms of Nehemiah (see Nehemiah 13), specifically, the attempt to purify the Israelite population, to reject foreign marriages and so on. Then if you ask if it would make sense in this period to compose a document that depicted the conquest the way Judges 1 does, you get a positive answer. By depicting the territories of Judah and Benjamin as those with the most uniform population of Israelites as opposed to foreigners, Judges 1 supports the agenda of Nehemiah's reform and the contemporary suspicion concerning "the people of the land" with whom the Jewish repatriates from Babylon quarreled (see Ezra 4:4, etc.).

So Judges 1 fits pretty well into that post-Exilic period. It could have been composed at that time and inserted into the older text of Joshua-Judges. I suspect that's the case, though I haven't found enough evidence to convince myself that it's certainly the case rather than what we've always thought. In any case, I hope the example raises the kind of issue that, as I'm sure my colleagues would agree, shows the peril we're in when we're doing biblical archaeology. When we're dealing with a literary text employing literary-critical criteria, our results don't correspond in a straightforward way with what we find, as Bill put, "on the ground." It may be that Judges 1 corresponds better with what Bill finds on the ground, but that correspondence may be an accident. Text-critically there's a lot of reason to think of Judges 1 as a document that's at least half a millennium too late to be relevant to the discussion of the early Iron Age. Does that seem to you to illustrate the complexity of the issue we're dealing with?

Hershel said to you that I work in all the various disciplines of our field. That was a very polite way of saying that I try to work as an amateur in the field. I play at archaeology and I play in the other areas. This variety gives me a perspective on the difficulty of comparing one of these issues to another. Let me paraphrase and partially quote a poem for you. It's a poem that belongs in the corpus of archaic Hebrew poetry. This is the corpus that Baruch Halpern emphasized to you as having special importance in our reconstruction of Israelite history and prehistory. The earliest portion in the biblical text that we can determine is the so-called archaic poetry, but the archaic Hebrew poem I'm going to talk about is not biblical. It was found at a site in the northern Sinai called Kuntillet Ajrud.* It is written in ink on plaster, on the wall of a building. The script is Phoenician rather than Hebrew, but the language is Hebrew. The site dates to the beginning of the ninth century B.C.E., but the poem belongs to the corpus of archaic Hebrew poetry because of its content and its nature, not because of the archaeological date of the site. Poetry is to be dated on the basis of established typologies of poetic form just as pottery is dated on the basis of ceramic typologies. On the basis of what we know of archaic Hebrew poetry, I would estimate that this poem, though it survives only in a ninth-century text, is probably an Iron I composition (1200-1000 B.C.E.).

The poem is very fragmentary, so I can't make it very elegant for you. It begins "When El shone forth . . . ," using the divine name El, which in the Bible is one of the names of the God of Israel and, as Bill pointed out earlier, is also a common name in the Canaanite pantheon for the king of the gods. "When El shone forth . . . ." The word I'm translating "shone forth" is a Hebrew verb that refers to the rising of the sun. Shining forth like sunrise is the image here. I don't want to suggest to you as our colleague Mark Smith from Yale would that there's solar imagery here, though I think Mark is certainly right that solar imagery is sometimes applied to the God of Israel in the Bible, and that scholars have given it too little attention.[2] The point here, however, is that the image the verb is drawing on in describing the appearance of El is sunrise, and that the sun rises, obviously, in the east.

A few lines after "When El shone forth" we read, continuing the same idea, "When Baal [arose] on the day of battle . . . ." The

---

* Suzanne Singer, "Cache of Hebrew and Phoenician Inscriptions Found in Desert," *Biblical Archaeology Review*, March 1976.

expression "on the day of battle" (*b'yom hammilchamah*) is strongly reminiscent of the biblical concept of "the day of Yahweh," which refers to a special event that the prophets looked forward to, a time when the God of Israel would arise in battle and defeat his enemies (see, for example, Isaiah 2:12-21, 13:6-10; Jeremiah 46:10; and Ezekiel 13:5). The use of the divine epithet Baal here, in combination with

---

Early Biblical Poetry that Reflects the Origins of Yahwism

Deuteronomy 33:2:
> Yahweh came from Sinai,
> He dawned from Seir,
> He appeared from Mount Paran.

Judges 5:4-5:
> Yahweh, when you went out from Seir,
> > When you marched from the fields of Edom,
> The earth shook,
> > Yes, the skies poured,
> > Yes, the clouds streamed with water.
> The mountains flowed before Yahweh,
> > the one of Sinai,
> Before Yahweh, the god of Israel.

Habakkuk 3:3,7:
> A god came from Teman,
> > A holy one from Mount Paran.
> His "splendor" covered the sky,
> His "praise" filled the earth. . . .
> The tents of Cushan quivered,
> > The curtains of the land of Midian shook.

Psalm 68:8-9:
> Yahweh, when you went out
> > in front of your people,
> > When you marched in Jeshimon,
> The earth shook,
> > Yes, the skies poured,
> Before Yahweh, the one of Sinai,
> > Before Yahweh, the god of Israel.

the fact that the script is Phoenician, has led some people to suggest that this is a Phoenician text and that there was a mixed population at Kuntillet Ajrud. Everyone recognizes that there was an Israelite presence there but they say there must also have been Phoenicians. But I don't really think so. I think that "Ba'al" here is simply an epithet meaning "lord." That's the common meaning of the Hebrew word *ba'al*, and there's very strong reason for believing that in early Israel, specifically during the early monarchy, the title or epithet "Ba'al" was an acceptable title for Yahweh. It was rejected later because it had so many associations with rival gods; in fact, *ba'al* eventually became a standard way of designating rival gods. But I think that the expression in the Kuntillet Ajrud poem simply means "When the lord [arose] on the day of battle."

In between the phrases "When El shone forth on the day of battle" and "When the lord [arose] on the day of battle" are verses describing the mountains melting in fear. The rest of the text is too fragmentary for reconstruction. (In one of my reconstructions there are six people riding on a single donkey [laughter]. I don't know what that might mean. I once corresponded with Professor Frank Cross of Harvard about this text and sent him that reading. He replied by saying that he didn't really have an opinion about the interpretation except that mine was almost certainly wrong. I agree. Six people riding on a donkey is a very uncomfortable reading. Especially for the donkey [laughter]. So I think that it's best to say the text breaks off.)

Now why do I describe to you such a poorly preserved text? The reason is that it represents an addition to this important corpus of poems that we have from the Bible, the archaic poetry. As I mentioned, this poetry has been identified as especially ancient on the basis of studies of poetic form. The corpus includes poems like Exodus 15, Judges 5, Deuteronomy 33, Habakkuk 3 and Psalm 68 (see box, p. 124). These and a few others constitute our earliest repertoire of biblical Hebrew poetry.

What do those poems have in common that might give us some information about the early worship of the God of Israel? What they say most consistently is that he is a warrior. He marches to battle against his enemies and on behalf of his people, and when he marches he comes from the southeast. He comes from Teman

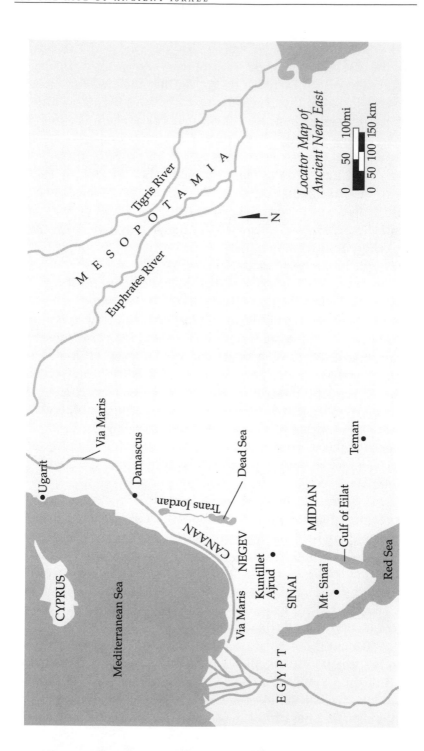

Locator Map of
Ancient Near East

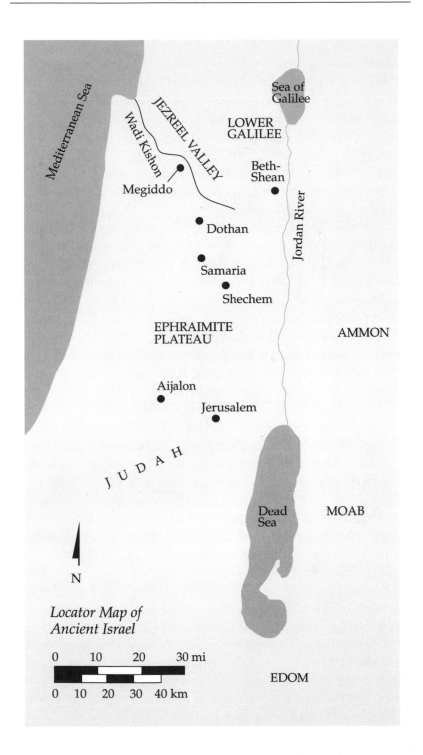

Locator Map of
Ancient Israel

(the southland) (Habakkuk 3:3) or from Edom (Judges 5:4), the country southeast of Judah, or from Sinai. Thus there is a series of geographical locations associated with this poetry that places the God of Israel in the earliest time that we can trace him to the south and east of historical Israel and Judah, and more specifically just to the east of the Wadi Arabah. Based on this observation and others, some scholars long ago concluded that somehow the worship of Yahweh, the God of Israel, had its origin south and east of Israel and Judah in the region which today includes the northern part of Saudi Arabia, southern Jordan and Israel.

Let me add some other reasons for revisiting this old idea. Theophany is a term that refers to an appearance or manifestation of a divine being. Mt. Sinai is the principal place of the theophany of Yahweh. Interestingly, this is true not only in the current form of the biblical story, but also in the early form of the tradition. Yahweh is associated with Sinai not only in Exodus 19, a relatively late passage that describes the arrival of the Exodus party at the mountain, but also in the earliest poetry, as we have seen. The persistence of the Sinai tradition is remarkable, because there was a natural tendency to eliminate it. That is, there was an understandable tendency to transfer the mountain location of the theophany of Yahweh to some place *within* the Promised Land, and specifically to Jerusalem. And, in fact, in the royal theology that grew up after the establishment of the Davidic dynasty, Mt. Zion was the sacred mountain. According to the Zion tradition, the Solomonic Temple was Yahweh's dwelling place forever (1 Kings 8:13). Why, then, didn't Mt. Zion displace Sinai altogether? The only explanation I know is that the old Sinai tradition was so venerable and well known, that it was so persistent and authentic, that it couldn't be suppressed.

Another indication that Yahwism originated south and east of Judah is the Midianite tradition. You remember that in the Exodus story Moses flees from Egypt into the wilderness and has his encounter with Yahweh. This momentous event takes place precisely in the region that we are talking about. The tradition was that the first encounter between Yahweh and the Israelites was in Midian, Midian being the name used in the Exodus story for this same region. This takes place in Exodus 2 and 3, where Moses marries the daughter of a man named Jethro. Jethro is a Midianite priest, and at one point (Exodus 18:11) Jethro says that Yahweh is the greatest of the gods. Exodus 6 shows that according to one part of the biblical tradition the God of Israel revealed his name Yahweh for the first time in Midian. In other words, even the Bible itself suggests that, in one sense, Yahwism originated south and east of Judah.

I want to back up into a discussion of the prehistory of Israel and Canaan, the subject that we've been talking about, because I don't think these subjects can be separated from one another. I would describe the process that Israel went through when it established itself in Canaan as a process of ethnic self-identification. It involved Israel's drawing boundary lines between itself and other peoples. This is why the question of where the increased Iron I population in the central hills came from is really a secondary issue in explaining Israelite origins. Wherever they came from—and I think their origin was diverse—they became a single people by drawing an ethnic boundary around themselves through the development of an elaborate genealogy.

An important part of this boundary drawing involved religion. The Israelites were those who worshiped Yahweh, the God of Israel. Similarly, the Ammonites were those who worshiped Milcom, the god of Ammon; the Moabites were those who worshiped Chemosh, the god of Moab; and the Edomites were those who worshiped Qaus, the god of Edom. Primary devotion to a chief national god was the characteristic pattern of the religions that developed in Iron Age Palestine. This suggests that Yahwism and Israel arose at the same time as a part of the same process. Let me explain

As we've seen, the setting of the prehistory of the Israelite community was the central hill country, which consists of highlands separated by a series of valleys. In the north is the Beth-Shean corridor that separates the hills of the Lower Galilee and Samaria via the Wadi Kishon and the Jezreel Valley. In the south is a series of valleys, including Aijalon, that separates the Samarian hills from those of Judah. It was in the upland region between these two valley systems that Israel emerged. As you've heard today, this region was very sparsely populated before 1200 B.C.E., and recent archaeological surveys have attempted to document the increase in population that began after 1200. One point that needs emphasis is that the boundaries of this region were dictated, I think, by Egyptian control of the major valleys and of the Via Maris or, as the Egyptians themselves called it, the Way of Horus—the road up the coastal plain. That road, which ran from Egypt across the northern Sinai, up the coastal plain of Palestine, through the Megiddo pass and onward to Damascus and points north, was a major route that the Egyptian empire needed to control for its own economic and political interests. This Egyptian control of the coastal plain and the major valleys had the effect of sealing in and isolating the central hill country. The small number of people who lived there lived in isolation from neighbors to the north, west and south.

At the end of the Late Bronze Age, events took place that led to the penetration of new people into the central hills. They settled in villages in the forests of the Ephraimite plateau in the east and north and in the saddle of Benjamin in the south. We've heard a lot today about where these people might have come from, and I find myself in general agreement with what Bill Dever told you. For a variety of reasons, life in the lowland cities was destabilized at this time, and there are a number of reasons for supposing that there was a substantial amount of movement out of those cities and into the central hills. If this is true, the movement was associated with a shift from an urban to a village lifestyle.* I suspect eventually we will learn that major fluctuations in weather were affecting this. When the weather becomes drier, it's more difficult to maintain large urban areas, and it's easier for people to live in villages. And there is some incidental evidence that in the last part of the Late Bronze Age the weather became increasingly and significantly drier in our region. The evidence is more than incidental for Mesopotamia, for which paleoclimatic studies have been done and published for the Late Bronze Age,[3] and corresponding changes in weather patterns in Europe during this period are well documented.[4] So it seems very likely that eventually we'll find that one important factor that was forcing people into rural settings was simply the inability of cities to sustain themselves in a drier period.

Many other factors contributed to the change of settlement patterns in Iron Age I, and you have heard about some of them today. The dramatic increase in population in the hills no longer

* Israel Finkelstein, "Searching for Israelite Origins," *Biblical Archaeology Review*, September/October 1988.

needs to be explained by positing an invasion. It's true, of course, that new people were arriving in Palestine.* The Philistines were arriving and other Sea Peoples were settling on the coastal plain at this time. But, at least in my opinion, their settlement was not so much the cause as one of the results of the change. We know that these Sea Peoples were in the eastern Mediterranean for some time before 1200. Much like the Vikings in northern Europe at a later time, they lived by raiding coastal villages, taking booty and sailing away. They had lived this way for centuries. Then circumstances changed, permitting them to settle down instead of plundering and running. The changed circumstances had weakened the large population areas to the point where they could no longer resist the attacks from the sea.

Egypt had become too weak to sustain an empire. The population in the large coastal cities and in the major cities of the valleys, such as Aijalon and Jezreel, began to decline. The cities began to collapse, and the nearby highlands began to fill up with new settlements and new villages. You've heard the word "Shasu" today, an Egyptian term for Asiatic nomads. Were there Shasu among the settlers in the hills? Yes, in all probability there were, though it's very difficult for archaeology to confirm the arrival of the occasional nomad.** And in any case, the Shasu don't seem to be the major element. To be sure, some of our colleagues in Germany still describe the population expansion in terms of Bedouin settling down and, as Bill pointed out, some Israeli scholars agree. But the old settlement theory, as expressed in classic form by the German scholar Albrecht Alt, has no more to recommend it today than the invasion or armed conquest theory, and the social revolution theory† has failed because of a total lack of supporting evidence. Instead, we now see the emergence of Israel as a complex phenomenon involving, first, the arrival of new peoples in the central hills from a variety of sources, including especially the collapsing cities of the Egypto-

---

* Trude Dothan, "What We Know About the Philistines," *Biblical Archaeology Review*, July/August 1982; "Ekron of the Philistines: Where They Came From, How They Settled Down and the Place They Worshiped In," *Biblical Archaeology Review*, January/February 1990.

** Steven A. Rosen, "Finding Evidence of Ancient Nomads," *Biblical Archaeology Review*, September/October 1988.

† "Israel's Emergence in Canaan—BR Interviews Norman Gottwald," *Bible Review*, October 1989.

Canaanite empire, and, second, the gradual process of ethnic self-identification that generated an elaborate genealogy linking the high-landers to each other.

This brings us to an interesting and extremely important fact. There was something called Israel in Canaan before all this happened. When I was trained in this field, I was taught that Merneptah's so-called Israel Stele, which you've heard about quite a bit today, was the key in dating the arrival of Israel in Canaan.* When the standard question of the conquest of Canaan was asked, the answer always invoked Merneptah's campaign late in the 13th century as a decisive *terminus ante quem*. Because the stele mentions Israel, the conquest must have taken place earlier. In view of our wealth of new information, however, Merneptah's stele now appears totally different in its significance, though no less important. Now that we know that the population of the central hills, which would become the heartland of Israel, burgeoned in the Iron I period *after* rather than before the date of Merneptah's campaign, we have to revise our understanding of the stele's significance completely. It shows us something quite different from what we thought before. It shows us that there was in Canaan something, some entity—some people who could be identified as Israel—*before* the changes that created what we usually think of as early Israel took place.

This point, then, is crucial. Somewhere in the sparsely populated hills of Late Bronze Age Canaan, there was a people called Israel. When newcomers settled in the hills in the subsequent period, at the beginning of the Iron Age, they allied themselves with this proto-Israelite group, and the eventual result was the formation of what we usually think of as early Israel, a group of tribes bound together by genealogical ties who would eventually evolve into a nation-state.

You may wonder what I mean by saying that new people arrived, affiliated with Israel and became Israelites. Israel was, after all, an ethnic group—a people united by kinship. So it might seem that someone either was or wasn't an Israelite. We can understand how a non-Israelite might affiliate with Israel politically or religiously, but could someone affiliate ethnically? The answer is yes. Kinship is, of

* Frank J. Yurco, "3,200-Year-Old Picture of Israelites Found in Egypt," *Biblical Archaeology Review*, September/October 1990.

course, defined by biology and expressed by genealogy. But in many societies specific relationships within a genealogy may be artificial from a strictly biological point of view. That is, factors other than biological descent often come into play. In most kinship systems, affiliation by marriage or adoption constitutes kinship. In some systems, there are other nonbiological ways in which kinship can be established. If you go to the social-scientific studies of ethnicity that have been done recently, you'll find that there is a strong interest in this subject. Researchers have studied populations around the world in an attempt to determine how groups of people identify themselves as kin over against other groups. There is a special interest in kinship groups who live alongside other groups in a mixed population. The question is, how do ethnic groups assert and sustain their identity? In a variety of ways ethnic groups draw boundaries around themselves. They may do this with religion or languages or accents or codes of dress or diet or a combination of these and other things. But in one way or another they draw boundaries around themselves. And this boundary-marking is what creates ethnicity.

A process went on in the Iron I period where a large population who had not previously been Israelite identified themselves with a small group that had previously been Israelite by a process of ethnic boundary-marking. When you read the Bible, you find evidence of this. The biblical writings frequently and persistently assert that the Israelites are not Canaanites and that the Israelites should not marry Canaanites. There's great emphasis in the Bible on family history and genealogy. All this comes out of a very long tradition of boundary-marking. It was that tradition that created Israel in the first place.

Interestingly enough, moreover, the boundary-marking created Israel not by total innovation but by identification with an existing people. Who were these proto-Israelites? Let me attempt to answer this question in the context of a hypothesis. In the Late Bronze Age, I suggest, there was a continuum of culture in the hinterlands of Palestine and Transjordan, the backwater region outside of the main lines (the coastal plain and major valleys) that were controlled by the Egyptian empire. This region extended in a crescent from Dothan and Shechem in the northern Samarian hills east into central Transjordan and south to the northeastern shores of the

Gulf of Eilat. These boundaries, again, were dictated by Egyptian control of the lowlands. The hinterlands, sealed on the north by the Beth-Shean corridor and on the south by the valley of Aijalon and the Negev, were isolated from the influence of the Egypto-Canaanite culture of the lowlands. The customs and ideas that developed during the Late Bronze Age in this isolated region are not the Canaanite culture that we are familiar with from reading the Canaanite texts from Ugarit or from the reports of the Egyptians and Hittites of their experience with the peoples of lowland Palestine.

As Bill explained, the archaeological surveys of Iron I sites in the hill country have revealed a wide distribution of distinctive Iron I pottery types that extends beyond the hills of Samaria and Judah into central and southern Transjordan, the region that would eventually become Ammon, Moab and Edom. The uniformity of this pottery tradition, together with other indications, suggests a common cultural background that is most easily explained as a consequence of a continuity throughout the region in the Late Bronze Age. Now, what I am suggesting to you is that in that period, the Late Bronze Age, the earliest characteristic aspects of Israelite culture developed, most especially the worship of the God of Israel. This is the only period in which the central hills of Palestine, where Yahwism took root, and the region northeast of the Gulf of Eilat, where Yahwism originated, were connected in a cultural continuum. After the rise of the nation-states of Ammon, Moab and Edom early in the Iron Age this continuum was brought to an end. Thus if Yahwism came to Israel from Midian, as it almost certainly did, it had to arise in the Late Bronze Age and not in the Iron Age.

All this suggests that the Israel that existed at the time of the Merneptah Stele was an Israel that was already Yahwistic. Thus the population that began to flow into the area where these proto-Israelites lived in the Iron Age allied itself with the religion as well as with the people. The traditions they embraced were strong enough that once the nation-states of Israel and Judah were created, they already had Yahwism as a basic component of their culture. Later, in the Iron II period, when Israel began to worship Yahweh of Samaria, as he's called in the Kuntillet Ajrud inscription, and Judah began to worship Yahweh-in-Zion, as he's called in the Book of Psalms, neither of those national religions was strong enough to eradicate the

"I HAVE BLESSED YOU BY YAHWEH OF SAMARIA AND HIS ASHERAH,"
declares the inscription at the top of this pottery fragment from Kuntillet Ajrud. The
identity of the three figures below the inscription has been the subject of heated debate
among scholars. Some take the figure at left to be a representation of Yahweh, with the
goddess Asherah depicted either at center or at right. These scholars argue that Asherah
was Yahweh's consort. Others see both the figure at left and at center to be the Egyptian
god Bes in his typical arms akimbo pose, topped by a feathered headdress; the figure at
right, in this view, is merely a lyre player. Kyle McCarter notes that the appellation
"Yahweh of Samaria" was used by those living in the kingdom of Israel after it had
split from Judah in the late tenth century B.C.E. In both states, McCarter emphasizes,
the powerful memory of the earlier Yahwistic religion, with its roots to the south and to
the east of the two kingdoms, lived on. It was this powerful faith, perhaps more than
anything else, that lay at the heart of Israelite origins.

memory of the proto-Israelite or pre-Israelite Yahwistic religion that, in a real sense, created the people and made possible the existence of the two countries.

ENDNOTES

1. Baruch Halpern, *The Emergence of Israel in Canaan* (Chico, CA: Scholars Press, 1983).

2. Mark Smith, *The Early History of God* (San Francisco: Harper & Row, 1990), pp. 115-124.

3. J. Neumann and S. Parpola, "Climatic Change and the Eleventh-Tenth Century Eclipse of Assyria and Babylonia," *Journal of Near Eastern Studies* 46 (1987), pp. 161-183.

4. The evidence is summarized in Neumann and Parpola's article, cited in note 3 above.

Questions & Answers

Reference is sometimes made to a consort of the God of Israel. Can you comment on that?

Yes, but it's such a complicated question I can't answer it in a sentence or two. The question has to do with the consort of the God of Israel. Is the God of Israel really a bachelor god or not? One of the things we learn from the Kuntillet Ajrud inscriptions is that there was a tradition of Israelite piety (and probably Judahite piety as well, since both the southern and northern kingdoms are represented at the site) that included the worship of a goddess alongside Yahweh.* So the short answer is: Yes, some Israelites in some historical periods believed that Yahweh had a consort.

But we shouldn't think of this Israelite goddess in quite the same way we think of the Canaanite goddesses of the Bronze Age pantheons. Yahwism, once it had arisen, had characteristics that differentiated it sharply from Bronze Age religion. Iron Age religion in Israel—and I think also in Ammon, Moab and Edom and probably in certain of the Aramean states—was not like Bronze Age religion. We know a lot about Bronze Age religion; we don't know much about Iron Age religion from primary sources. We know it only filtered through biblical writers who after all were writing from a perspective of a fully developed monotheism, which came later. But as I would reconstruct it, the official religion practiced in the capital cities of Israel and Judah in the ninth century B.C.E. saw Yahweh in conjunction with a consort who was the personification of his cultically available presence.

What does that mean? If you go into a church or a synagogue or a temple, you say the presence of God is here. Now in certain periods in antiquity the cultic presence of a god worshiped in a given shrine is attributed substance. The technical term for the substantial form of an abstract concept such as cultic presence is "hypostasis." Sometimes the hypostatized form of a deity's cultic presence is personified. When it's the presence of a male deity, the hypostasis is

* Ze'ev Meshel, "Did Yahweh Have a Consort?" *Biblical Archaeology Review*, March/April 1979; André Lemaire, "Who or What Was Yahweh's Asherah?" *Biblical Archaeology Review*, November/December 1984.

characteristically personified as a female deity. My interpretation of
the question of the consort at Kuntillet Ajrud is that she was the
personified form of the hypostatized presence of Yahweh. To put it
differently: She was the available medium through whom you invoked him. And she was also thought of as his consort. And so, yes,
we now know that the God of Israel in some circles was not regarded
as a bachelor.

Of course, we should have known that already, because the
biblical prophets, who didn't approve of the arrangement, frequently
use language that implies that the Israelites were worshiping a goddess, and the historical books of the Bible say explicitly that the kings
of Israel and Judah worshiped the Asherah. There was a stream of
religion that rejected the goddess, however, and that stream finally
vindicated itself in the form of Yahwism that became Judaism, so
that Judaism became a religion that permitted no plurality, even a
male-female duality, in the deity. That's why the idea of an Israelite
goddess seems alien to us, whereas in the Iron Age it was a fixed
feature of the religion—at least in certain circles.

**Just who are the Philistines, according to what we know now? Are
they Mycenaean or Greeks or something else?**

They are one of the peoples who appear in the eastern Mediterranean at the end of the Late Bronze Age. They are first referred to by
the name Philistine—Peleshet or Pereshet—in Egyptian sources, and
are commonly mentioned in the documents of Ramesses III, who
flourished in the second quarter of 12th century B.C.E. They settled
down on the coastal plain of Canaan, south of the Carmel spur,
which became known as the Philistine Plain. Later their name became one of the names for the whole country—Palestine. According
to biblical tradition, the Philistines came originally from Crete—
biblical Caphtor. In all probability, this tradition reflects historical
reality. Scholars have found iconographic evidence and other reasons to connect the ancestors of the Philistines with Crete. One of
the peoples mentioned in the Bible as close neighbors to the Philistines are the Cherethites, a group of whom became mercenaries in
King David's personal bodyguard, and a likely interpretation of the
term Cherethites is that it derives from Crete.

In light of your comments on the presence of God—the hypostasis—could you connect that with the findings in the Jewish temple that was found in the island of Elephantine in the Nile. I believe the shrine there was devoted to Yahweh and two goddesses.

There are Aramaic documents from the Persian period that preserve correspondence between a Jewish community on an island in the Nile, called Elephantine Island, and Jerusalem. That is, we have correspondence between the main Jewish community and an Egyptian Jewish colony, in effect. These documents show that the Elephantine community had not only temples to Yahweh, whom they called Yaho, but also a number of other deities who seem to be Jewish and which have aspects of Yahweh in their names. A long time ago, Albright suggested that the other deities were aspects of Yahweh, rather than syncretistic deities from other religions. I subscribe to that idea. I think Albright was right about that. He had a clear perception of the complexity of reconstructing religious forms that we're not familiar with. I think it's too simplistic, as I've already said, to say there's Canaanite religion, there's monotheism and then there's syncretism. There's a whole set of religious ideas in between that we need to describe. The Elephantine documents provided our first clue. They are a primary source for interpreting the Kuntillet Ajrud material.

Would you consider Psalm 29 in that early genre?

Yes. Although I failed to mention it, I absolutely would include Psalm 29 in the corpus of archaic poetry.

I have great trepidation in asking this because I'm afraid I'm going in the face of tremendous scholarship. But the conquest hypothesis seems to be pretty much defunct at this point. Yet, if you consider the Bible to be something that's trying to establish the pedigree of the people and the title to the land, wouldn't it have been to the advantage of the authors or the redactor to have said, "Yes, we arose from an indigenous population and hence have a pretty clear claim to the land," rather than saying "we are intruders from the outside who have conquered it by the sword"?

Since I was talking about religion, I really didn't have a chance to say much about the conquest hypothesis, and I'm happy to have an opportunity to do so. I described the situation as I understood it: A new population came into a geographically isolated area and affiliated with an ethnic and religious community that was already there. As the highland population became increasingly numerous and the cities in the lowlands became increasingly vulnerable, there eventually and inevitably came a time of conflict. The people in the hinterlands conquered the lowland cities—not in one great campaign, but one after another over an extended period of time. We can date the process reasonably. We know, for example, that Beth-Shean held out as an Egypto-Canaanite city until at least the time of Ramesses VI (1141-1134 B.C.E.), whose name appears on a scarab found there. We know from the Bible that Jerusalem remained independent until the time of David. But eventually these cities fell to Israelite conquerors. What I would suggest is that it is the memory of the victories against these cities and their capture by the Israelites in streamlined form that created the tradition behind the Book of Joshua. I think the conquest in the Joshua story is not a historical document at all, but a religious confession having to do with the sacrality of the Promised Land. Nevertheless, I think it contains within it a tradition that goes back to historical battles and the actual conquest of lowland cities by Israelites. In short, I wouldn't abandon the conquest model altogether, because I do think that the conquest stories include a recollection of actual military activity.

I'm curious to know if the scholars have any opinion about what happened to the Israelite kingdom when the Assyrians removed them from the land.

It's a very interesting subject—the legends of the ten lost tribes. What happened to the northern population of Israel is what happened to most of the world during that period. At the time the Assyrian policy of deportation of populations, of moving significant numbers of people from one place to another, was at least in part for the purpose of trying to destroy their sense of political identity and territory. It's one of those terrible things that people have done to each other in human history. The Assyrians had the perception, which unfortunately is in a way grimly accurate, that if you take a people out of their own land they are less likely to rebel against you. They lose their sense of identity, they meld into the new population. And it worked.

Where did they go?

We're told where they went. They were moved to the locations of other peoples. They were moved up into Syria. They were moved over into Mesopotamia. They were moved all over—and they disappeared. I don't think they reemerged as the Cherokees or Anglo-Saxons. Once they were taken away, they lost their identity. The peoples that moved in adopted the identity of the new location. The legend of the lost tribes, as a part of post-biblical folklore, is a subject that really lies outside our kind of expertise.

Panel Discussion

Hershel Shanks: When you fellows address one another it seems to me you have been too polite. (Laughter.) There seems too much, "Oh, what this one said was so right" and "I agree with that one who was so right." There were some vigorous disagreements, but all with scholars who weren't here—Israel Finkelstein, Norman Gottwald, Adam Zertal. So when we evaluate these comments expressing agreement, we have to remember that there have been disagreements with people who aren't here to defend themselves.

As I listened to you, Bill [Dever], I thought that there was much that Baruch [Halpern] would disagree with, but I was sitting next to him as you spoke and I saw him nodding his head, yes, in agreement with you. (Laughter.) Let me ask our audience: If you were convinced by Bill Dever, raise your hand. How many were convinced by him? (Laughter.) And how many were not convinced by him? Well, I would say it's two to one in Bill's favor.

I would like to open the discussion by asking the panelists if they would address their differences. I would also like to ask a specific question. In some respects we credit the biblical text. The biblical text says that Jerusalem wasn't conquered until the time of David. It became Israelite only in the time of David. This is a kind of admission; you would think, if they were making up stories, they would claim an earlier victory, although it does say in Joshua that there apparently was a battle for Jerusalem that the Israelites won earlier. It is clear that that tradition did not prevail. So one asks why the biblical writers have to be so dishonest about the other sites. I'm not quite as ready to dismiss biblical text as some. We have to make distinctions within the biblical text. I also want to raise a question about the Merneptah Stele, which seems to be a critical part of the discussion. Except for that, I think it would be much easier to conclude that there was no Israel prior to 1200 B.C.E.

Kyle [McCarter] said that when he was in graduate school the Merneptah Stele was taken to indicate that this was the latest date Israel could be in Canaan. Now that's not true; Israel is just emerging in 1200 B.C.E. Yet you do have a situation where, archaeologically, you have this new population coming in, beginning in about 1200 B.C.E., and yet you have an Egyptian stele that says that there was a people there earlier, namely Israel. But Kyle says it was a different kind of people, not the Israel we know later. I want to know what defined this earlier people. Was it religion? What defined their ethnicity? We have all these different markers that were mentioned—dress, food, religion, etc. It seems we have two Israels—at least, according to this theory—one Israel, the pre-Merneptah Israel; the other, the post-Iron Age Israel that the archaeological evidence attests to. I'll stop here and ask our panelists to comment and see if there's any disagreement among them.

William Dever: I want to jump in immediately. You invented a problem that doesn't exist. (Laughter.) I can therefore solve it easily. We are trying to be too fine-tuned in our chronology. When we say around 1200 B.C.E., that's really what we mean. I think both you and Kyle will get off the hook easily, because there is no problem at all in dating the earliest of these settlements around 1230 or 1225 B.C.E. All archaeologists would agree. The pottery is still strongly in the Late Bronze 13th-century tradition. There are even a few Mycenaean sherds—of the Mycenaean IIIB type—around. So when we say around 1200 B.C.E., don't take that too literally. The fact is that there is no problem archaeologically in saying that by the time of Merneptah these so-called Israelite settlements were at least 20 to

30 years old. That's enough time for them to be established and for them to establish these all-important boundaries you're talking about. There's really plenty of time. So it's really a semantic problem. It's easily solved.

Shanks: How? (Laughter.)

Dever: There aren't two Israels. There's only one. Because if you begin the process a little earlier, then you have time for this development to take place. It doesn't need to be compressed.

Kyle McCarter: The point is, though—and I think this is probably something we can all agree on (laughter), there is an increasing number of people who belong to Israel. It's not as if you have Israelites coming in. The question is, you start with a smaller group—I'm not saying there are two Israels; I never would suggest that—I'm saying there was a smaller group of people who were Israel and the question . . .

Shanks: Where were they? Were they in the cities?

McCarter: No, they were in the hills.

Dever: Some of them can be in these new villages, which can be that early.

McCarter: That's right. The question we should be studying and trying to understand better is what the process was by which people who had not formerly understood themselves to be Israelites became Israelites.

Dever: Exactly.

McCarter: That's the process of ethnic identification. It's a subject we have not dealt with very much in our field, but it's been generously dealt with in other fields. We can learn from our colleagues, for example, the [Paul] Lapps and others, what is involved trying to develop and maintain an ethnic identity.

Dever: But the challenge here—and we archaeologists recognize it—is how to trace ethnicity in material culture, in the archaeological record. What kinds of behavioral traits survive? I'm suggesting that things like house form do survive and that they have certain implications for social and family structure. Other things do not survive and, as I indicated, one of the things that unfortunately does not seem to survive well is religious behavior. We have few artifacts in these settlement sites that are explicitly religious in character. That does not mean for a moment that religion was not a major factor. I suspect it was. But archaeologically, we cannot yet comment. The lack of any kinds of temples or shrines itself may be significant. It may mean that Yahwism, which I believe existed very early, was still not crystallized. There was not an official priesthood. There were not sanctuaries in which one could worship. If the common, ordinary, everyday Israelite could say prayers and offer sacrifices almost anywhere, then nothing would survive for us to find. The silence of the archaeological record may not mean anything, however. It may not be evidence for or against an ideology such as you suggest.

McCarter: Hershel, there was an issue that came up today that I didn't agree with. Something that Baruch [Halpern] said addresses a very important issue in the field and it's something that's been treated very often. I have what I think is a minority opinion, but let me express it. It has to do with the question of the 'Apiru. Who were the 'Apiru? There has been a very popular theory in the field for years and years to identify the 'Apiru with the *ivrim*, the Hebrews. It is assumed that they are somehow the same word, that the old social group term for 'Apiru became transformed into an ethnic term, namely "Hebrew." I don't think that's right. I think the evidence is really on the other side. I got the impression from what Baruch said that he thinks it *is* right.

I agree that we have learned a lot about early Israel from studying the 'Apiru phenomenon, but I don't think that means that the term is the same. Let me explain. As best we can understand, the term "'Apiru" is a very, very widespread term; it's not just Egyptian. In fact, I think it was only secondarily Egyptian. I think that it is a North West Semitic term that was also used in Mesopotamia. It refers to any people in a client relationship to another people. The

'Apiru were hired by somebody else to do something. That may mean military, it may mean household servants, it can mean all sorts of things. But the verbal root seems to mean client.

We have a whole series of names that were popular at one period in the second millennium B.C.E. that included the word "'Apiru," combined with a divine name. A name like Apir-dagan meant the client of the god Dagan. 'Apiru were clients. There is usually a negative connotation to the term in that they were sort of the riffraff, people who sold themselves into the service of somebody else—mercenaries, in other words. But it's not always a negative thing and I think—even though this will sound very naive to my colleagues and to many of you—I still think we have a good etymology for the word Hebrew.

I think the biblical tradition is unanimous in saying that the one thing you can say about "Hebrew" is that it's an ethnic term. The term *B'nai Israel* (Israelites), is both ethnic, national and political, but *ivrim* (Hebrews) is always ethnic in the Bible. The one thing that the Israelites say about themselves ethnically is that we are not Canaanites. We came from Mesopotamia. We came from Trans-Euphrates. The word "trans" is the word *ever*. In the 19th century, biblical scholars assumed that the word "Hebrew" came from the word *ever*—"across"; that is, the people who come from across there, rather than from here. I still think that's true. I think people were right 100 years ago about this. I think the clever idea to associate Hebrew with the 'Apiru is not right. It made more sense when we thought it was *Habiru*, because then we had *ayin, b, r* instead of *ayin, p, r*, but now I don't think it's right. So tell me why I'm wrong. (Laughter.)

Baruch Halpern: I'm inclined to agree. (Laughter.)

McCarter: That's not what you said.

Halpern: Actually, where I would nuance that is that what Kyle said could be right as far as it goes. "'Apiru" is not an ethnicon as it's used in second millennium sources. *Ivri*, Hebrew, is an ethnic term in biblical sources. (It does not appear outside of biblical sources.) In biblical sources, *ivri* is a term that applies to a large group of people.

They are all descendants of an eponymous *Ever* in the biblical ethnology, taking in everybody running from Yemen all the way up to central Syria and even to the Euphrates. Is this an ethnic group or not? And if it is an ethnic group—it is the name of an ethnic group in the Bible and only in the Bible—it is only in the mind. Ethnicity is something that is only in the mind; it is an ideology. Only in Israelite ideology is this an ethnic group.

Does this ethnic group derive its name from a term that probably means "client"? (I wouldn't necessarily agree that it means only client. In its second millennium B.C.E. use, it is represented by a term for bandit—when it is written in Akkadian, for the most part.) Secondly, it is used of people who are severed from their kinship links and then attached to somebody else's service. Now the real question concerns the transition—the relationship between how a term referring to social status could be related to a term for an ethnic group. The difficulty with this isn't primarily linguistic because the Akkadian syllabic writing of "Habiru" is always with a *b* sign, never with a *p1* sign, which suggests to me you have interchange of *b* and *p* across linguistic boundaries.

Shanks: I think we better not go any deeper into that or we're going to lose everybody. (Laughter.)

Halpern: I didn't mean to go any deeper into that. At that juncture you have a choice to make. Is this an originally ethnic term which, because of the nature of the ethnic group, was turned into a sociological term, but which, nevertheless, among a certain group maintained its ethnic connotations? Was this a sociological term that, because of it's applicability to a certain group of people and their lifestyle, turned into an ethnic term? Or is there no relationship? I was just parroting old scholarship when I made my remarks, and I think it's perfectly legitimate to question the relationship between the two. In fact, Kyle's in good company with a number of very talented German scholars.

Shanks: Bill [Dever] wants to challenge Kyle [McCarter] he whispers to me, so I'm going to let him.

Dever: Kyle and I have a token disagreement, at least. By the way, we didn't go to school together, I am much older than both of them put together. (Laughter.) But Kyle talked about the role of religion as a critical role and as I remember he was saying precisely, it was the religion that created the people. I would argue just the opposite, it was the people who created the religion.

Before Yahwism emerged, you probably had this sense of ethnicity. It need not have been fundamentally religious at all. I think we tend to project back onto the Bible our own feeling that religion has somehow got to be involved. As an archaeologist who deals with material culture remains, but who tries to appreciate the text of the Bible, I would argue that such solidarity as these highland frontier people had was probably largely social and economic—the necessity for survival. Yahwism emerged later as a kind of rationalization of their own experience and explanation for what they had gone through, and therefore Yahwism continued to develop and evolve, as it does within the Hebrew Bible itself. There's a frank admission of that. But it's like the chicken-and-egg argument: Which came first, Yahwism or Israel? Basically, as far as it is a chicken-and-egg argument, it is insoluble.

Shanks: Let me ask this question, then I'll throw it open to the audience. I hear you agree with one another that the major source of Israelites was the urban culture of the Late Bronze Age.

Dever: I wouldn't say urban. I would say more amongst the rural population. The one thing we do all agree on—I think almost everyone does—is that somehow most of the early Israelites, or proto-Israelites, were indigenous Canaanites. We cannot say exactly where they came from in Canaan—and remember that Transjordan was also part of Canaan. So if you want to derive some of them from the Jordan Valley and Transjordan, that's not outside of Canaan after all. But the indigenous business is what I think virtually everybody agrees on today.

Halpern: The exception I would take to that is the tradition of allochthony—that they, the Israelites, came from outside the country. Moreover, there is a strong streak of local xenophobia present in the earliest Israelite poetry. What I would conclude is that while no doubt a significant number of Israelites came from inside the country, the decisive influx must have come from outside. I would assume this for a variety of reasons, among them the depletion of manpower in Late Bronze Canaan, particularly at the end of the Late Bronze Age in Canaan. The 75,000 people that Bill places in the central hill country in Iron I—I would say it's more like 30,000 to 50,000 immigrants into the hill country—a significant portion of the people must have been allochthonous, people who came in from outside. That's why I want to get those Hebrews coming down from Syria.

Dever: Now you've got a problem. You've got a problem. Now both of you have a problem. If you want to derive them from central and southern Transjordan, you have no archaeological background. Even the so-called biblical sites like Heshbon, Dibon and others mentioned in the tradition were not occupied—any of them—before the 12th century and mostly not before the 11th century B.C.E. There's a vacuum, an archaeological vacuum, despite years of survey and excavation work in all of central and southern Transjordan. There is no place for these Israelites you talk about to have come from. And there is no trace of any Transjordanian elements in the material culture of the hill-country settlements. That's the problem with that view. I myself am sympathetic to it, but archaeologically we don't have any material to substantiate it.

Shanks: But you do agree with Kyle that the sources of Yahwism came from southeast of Judah and it had to come in the Late Bronze Age, before these ethnic groups coalesced.

Dever: It would be easier to argue, if you want to derive the religious traditions from that area, to put them down in the Iron Age because that's when you have settlement patterns that fit. In the 13th century B.C.E., the whole of southern Transjordan is a blank.

Shanks: But doesn't it seem difficult to get all these people coming out of an indigenous Canaanite location into the hill country and then bringing their religion from southeast of Judah?

Dever: I don't think they did, that's the point. And furthermore, I never said all of them were indigenous. I said the majority of them were. I do think that Yahwism comes into the tradition early—from somewhere, perhaps outside of central Palestine. But where it comes from does pose a problem for us archaeologically.

McCarter: Bill, let me press you a little bit on what you said about Transjordan being a blank.

Dever: In the south.

McCarter: Northern Transjordan is not a blank.

Dever: No.

McCarter: I was talking about down in the Hejaz. I was not talking about what is later Moab, but about much farther south. And that's not a blank, is it?

Dever: The problem is that very little archaeological work has been done in Saudi Arabia.

McCarter: What about the so-called Midianite culture?

Dever: Trenches have been dug recently, but not . . . All we have is a ceramic tradition. We do have a kind of ceramic tradition that could fit into the 13th or 12th century.

McCarter: I'm sorry, say that again.

Dever: We have a kind of tradition of painted pottery that many people think may be from east of . . .

McCarter: But there were probably people making that pottery. (Laughter.)

Dever: Yes, but we don't have sites from which you can derive any sizable groups of people. But of course the thing to remember always about archaeological arguments is they can be based on silence and then you have the one ugly sherd that kills the elegant theory.

McCarter: I just want to make sure that I wasn't understood to say that I thought the Israelites came from down there. I think the religion came from contacts down there. I don't assume there needed to be a large population to have this effect.

Dever: You can have pastoral nomadic peoples in movement who don't leave much trace, and ideas can diffuse in that way. There's no problem with that.

Shanks: Bill, I want to ask you about a statement you made about the cisterns and their importance in Iron I. Recently, it's been said that that argument is baseless, that, in fact, there are cisterns much earlier and that when you look at the hill-country sites you find very few of them with cisterns. In fact, the collared-rim jar was used to transport water from the springs to the houses.

Dever: Perhaps, but then I would be the archbishop of York. I don't think for a moment you can substantiate that. The fact is that there were cisterns earlier, but they were not common. And they were not necessarily a basic part of the technology. When you come to these Iron Age villages, cisterns were absolutely essential. Without storing water, you cannot settle the hill country. And so they developed simultaneously—these early Israelite villages and the widespread and sophisticated use of cisterns. Not that there aren't examples earlier; of course there are. Albright was wrong about that. As far as saying that there were no cisterns in these 300 settlement sites—does anything bother you about that statement? These are surface surveys we are discussing; they are not excavations. You're not going to find cisterns walking around on the surface of the ground—and, if you do, you can't date them. You must excavate them and see them in context. It is a fact that sites like Raddana and Ai and others that have been excavated do show consistent use of cisterns. So that's a bogus argument. As far as the use of collared-rim storage jars to carry water, it's possible, but you have to imagine a small donkey with two of these enormous jars on his back, each filled with water. It would weigh a couple hundred pounds. I'm not sure water was transported in that way. Nor would it have been necessary when you have springs close by, and with cisterns you don't need this. The jars were probably used for a variety of things, but I think more for storage than transport.

Shanks: All right, let's throw the discussion open to the audience . . .

I was somewhat confused by the sample of writing that we saw and I wonder if you would put it a little bit into perspective? You showed us a sample of writing from left to right that looked something like our Roman alphabet among the Canaanites at the same time that the Israelites were developing a right-to-left alphabet in exactly the same territory. That's my dilemma.

McCarter: The alphabet was invented in the region we are talking about today sometime in the middle of the second millennium. So the alphabet you saw on the screen had several centuries of tradition behind it. When it was invented, it could be written from right to left or from left to right or from up to down or in a form that we call boustrophedon (as the ox plows), where you start writing one way and when you get to the end of the line you turn around and go back the other way. At the time this abecedary was written at 'Izbet Sartah, it was an option to write from left to right, which is what that scribe did. It might have been the other way because at that time you could write in either direction.

What was the relationship of that to the Hebrew alphabet?

McCarter: All true alphabets are descended from the alphabet that was invented somewhere in Syria-Palestine the middle of the second millennium B.C.E. The 'Izbet Sartah ostracon is an example of what we call the paleo-Canaanite alphabet, the earliest form of the alphabet. It was probably a lot more complex than we know because most examples haven't survived. Once you get into the Iron Age and more specifically the Iron II period . . . once you get into the first millennium B.C.E., you get the rise of nation-states—Israel, Moab, Ammon, Philistia, Phoenicia—those nation-states tended to specialize the alphabet into national scripts, just as their languages developed into national languages and their religions developed into religions of national gods. At that time, the Hebrew alphabet developed as a special branch, but at 'Izbet Sartah it's too early to call that Hebrew or Phoenician. It's simply a North West Semitic alphabet. In fact even the famous Gezer calendar, from the tenth century B.C.E., found at Tell Gezer and supposedly a Hebrew inscription—it's not correct to call that a Hebrew alphabet. It's too early. The tenth century is still too early to say that this is Hebrew script, distinct from the other national scripts.

Dr. Dever, I think you argued that the proto-Israelites could have been settled in their mishpachot *(extended family settlements)—some 300 of these settlements—by the time of the Merneptah Stele. In what way, would anybody know to call them Israelite or the people of Israel?*

Dever: That's an absolutely fundamental question. I suggest two reasons: First, the biblical textual tradition itself, which one can project back that far. But I did stress that this proto-Israel is not the same as the "All Israel" of the later monarchical period. I suggested only that these are the progenitors of the later people . . .

But who did the Egyptian scribe have in mind when he wrote in the Merneptah Stele, *"Israel is destroyed, his seed is not"?*

Dever: That's the other reason—the Merneptah Stele itself. I would admit that without the Merneptah Stele—this extra-biblical reference to Israel—I'm not sure I would use the ethnic label of this time. I would be suspicious about pushing the biblical text quite that far back, but happily we do have the inscription. The meaning is perfectly clear to Egyptologists and to most historians. I mean it's perverse to argue, as a few do, that we can't read the inscription or that we don't know where or what Israel is. We do! And the date is clear—astronomically fixed, after all. So this is a priceless bit of textual evidence that allows us to attach the label "Israel" or "proto-Israel" to these sites. Without that I would be very cautious.

What you're saying is that by this early date they were already widely known and they themselves called themselves the people of Israel.

Dever: Precisely, and that is warrant enough. If they called themselves Israelites, I think we can.

I mean what else would anybody else call them. This was not a common epithet or anything.

Dever: No, but it was common enough for the Egyptians to have known about it and used it. And we know from previous inscriptions that Egyptian intelligence about Palestine was usually pretty good. Therefore, on that basis, I think we can use the term "Israel," but I do put it in quotes because I want to be careful of closing the argument until we have more evidence, but the evidence is coming steadily from archaeological investigations.

Again, Dr. Dever, it seems a little strange to me that if, at the time of the Merneptah Stele, Israel was simply a conglomeration of hill people, why would Merneptah, a great king of Egypt, spend extra time to say his [Israel's] seed is destroyed? That to me indicates perhaps there was something special about the Israelites at that time that the Egyptian pharaoh wanted to point out—that he was responsible for its destruction.

My second point is: It seems everybody, the entire panel, accepts the chronology. I was just wondering, is there any academic ferment about the chronology? Is it subject to question?

Dever: Both good questions. As far as the latter question is concerned, there is some small dispute amongst historians—mainly between Egyptologists and Palestinian archaeologists. But there's no more than about a 20-year margin of error. That's why the Merneptah Stele used to be dated as early as about 1230 B.C.E.; today it's dated about 1207 B.C.E. Twenty years is not a great margin of error. That's all. We've got it down to 20 years. There are no other chronological problems. We're that close to absolute calendar dates. So the chronological issue is a modest one and it's not going to make much difference.

Your first question had to do with the text of the stele. We didn't read all of the text earlier and we should have, because Israel is not the only people claimed to have been conquered in this inscription—only one of several. Here's the whole pertinent part: "Canaan has been plundered into every sort of woe, Ashkelon has been overcome, Gezer has been captured, Yanoam has been made nonexistent, Israel is laid waste, his seed is not." So Israel is not singled out; on the contrary.

Halpern: I'd beg to differ here, because the continuation of the inscription which was not read says that "Hurru is made a widow for Egypt." That is a couplet with the line, "Israel is laid waste, his seed is not." With the loss of Israel's insemination, Hurru has become a widow for Egypt. Hurru is a generic term for Canaan. I suggest that what we have is an image of the Israelites entering, in some number, the hill country of Canaan and thus fructifying it. I think Israel is being singled out not just in that sense, but also by the determinative that is used with respect to it. I don't think it makes Israel politically more important than anybody else; it's just that it's a phenomenon; it's something unusual, something unexpected.

Shanks: Baruch, if I understood the question correctly, what he wants to know is why is a bunch of rural agriculturalists so significant to the pharaoh?

Halpern: Because he could claim a victory over them. (Laughter.)

Dever: The Shasu are also mentioned. Why mention a bunch of ragged sheepherders in Transjordan? But the Egyptians did mention them. Another thing needs to be said: You can doubt the historical veracity of words of an inscription; maybe it was just typical Egyptian boasting, but maybe not. For instance, at Gezer we have a destruction level; there is nothing in the biblical tradition to suggest that the Israelites destroyed Gezer, nor the Sea Peoples—the Philistines. Some years ago we published substantial evidence to show that Merneptah was not altogether boasting. Gezer did suffer a destruction that we dated on independent grounds somewhere just before 1200 B.C.E. Ashkelon is now being excavated; the excavator there, Larry Stager, thinks he can also date a Merneptah destruction, so perhaps the inscription is not just a boast.

Halpern: Yes, there are good grounds at Ashkelon for this.

I have a question for each of you. I've heard it claimed by some Palestinian leaders that they have more of a claim to Palestine, the state of Israel, whatever term you want to use, because they are really descended from the Canaanites who were there preceding the Israelites—that is to say, preceding the Hebrews. Does your research shed any light to support that claim or to deny that claim or are you unable to comment on that?

Dever: I have a plane to catch. (Laughter.) Basically we're antiquarians. We're not experts on the modern situation in the Middle East. I lived there 12 years, which means I know almost nothing. Ask a tourist who's been there three weeks—they know everything. (Laughter.) Ask Mr. Bush. He seems to know a lot of things (laughter); but they aren't true. I don't want to be facetious, but in fact all you can say is that the peoples in this present area are so mixed culturally, ethnically and racially over such long periods of time that any kind of historical claim advanced by either side is nonsense.

Halpern: There's one clear claim on precedence for the ownership of that country and it belongs to Cro-Magnon man. (Laughter.) Subsequently it developed that they intermarried with the Neanderthals, when the process Bill is talking about began.

McCarter: I think the thing to remember is that not only the Jewish but the Islamic inhabitants of that region have a long traditional attachment to the stories of Abraham. And so they both trace their claim to Abrahamic traditions. Those are traditions of a religious nature, traditions that we can study but that we can't evaluate or take sides on. And I think that what you hear when you hear Palestinians making a greater claim—this is because of the fact that Islam is an Abrahamic religion, just as Judaism is. And so from the Palestinian point of view they have a very firm and very ancient claim to the land that belonged to Ishmael. The Jews, by the same logic and argument, have a claim to the land that belonged to Isaac and Jacob. That's really something that you can appreciate and admire; you like the idea that people have long-standing claims and understand their traditions. On the other hand, what it really helps you do is to appreciate how difficult the situation in the region is and why the lines of disagreement are so deep and so sincere on both sides.

Dever: I would like to add just a word about archaeology. Archaeology, unfortunately, does get involved in the political struggles in the Middle East. Most of us try to resist that, particularly we Americans who are working both in Israel and Jordan. I have students working in both Israel and Jordan. I really have a fine line to walk. But it's very easy to abuse archaeological evidence in the interest of nationalism—and absolutely fatal. The combination of nationalism and religion—and the kind of extremism you get in the Middle East in the service of archaeology . . . ah! Remember what the Nazis did in the name of archaeology—the super culture! Very dangerous.

Shanks: One more question and it's yours.

So much has changed in the last ten years. The last time I read a book on what we're talking about today, Abraham was considered to be a historical figure. You said that ivrim *was not the source of the word Hebrew, that it was* ever, *which means "across," "coming from across." Is that related to Abraham (Avraham in Hebrew)?*

McCarter: Even though in English Abraham (which is Avraham in Hebrew) and *ever* may sound alike, they are actually quite different. The consonants are completely different in the ancient languages. So Abraham can't be related to the word Hebrew. It's not possible.

Shanks: You've been a wonderful audience. You've stuck with us through the whole day. We hope you've enjoyed it as much as we have. Thank you.

Photo Credits

Front Cover: Zev Radovan

Color plate I: Hershel Shanks; *color plate II:* Erich Lessing; *color plate III:* Jurgen Liepe; *color plate IV:* Adam Zertal; *color plate V:* Judith Dekel; *color plate VI:* Joseph Callaway

P. viii: (top) Beverly Rezneck; *p. ix:* (top) Lori Stiles, (bottom) Bob Stockfield

P. 4: courtesy the Union Theological Seminary Archives, The Burke Library, NYC; *p. 8:* Israel Finkelstein, *The Archaeology of the Israelite Settlement,* Israel Exploration Society; *p. 10:* courtesy of Israel Finkelstein; *p. 18:* Jurgen Liepe; *p. 20:* (photo) Frank Yurco, *Journal of The American Research Center in Egypt* 23, 1986; (drawing) Paul Hoffman/F. Schonbach; *p. 21:* (photo) Frank Yurco; (drawing) F. Schonbach; *p. 33:* Hebrew University of Jerusalem; *p. 34:* Israel Antiquities Authority/Israel Museum; *p. 36:* Joint Expedition to Ai; *p. 37:* Joseph Callaway; *p. 39* (photo) Joseph Callaway; (drawing) Lawrence E. Stager; *p. 41:* David Harris/Israel Museum/Israel Antiquities Authority; *p. 42:* Joseph Callaway; *p. 45:* Israel Finkelstein, *The Archaeology of the Israelite Settlement,* Israel Exploration Society; *p. 47:* Moshe Kochavi; *p. 95:* Manfred Bietak; *p. 96:* Sipa Press/Art Resource, NY; *p. 98:* Israel Antiquities Authority; *p. 100:* Staatliche Museun, Berlin; *p. 135:* (photo) Avraham Hai, (drawing) after Perhiya Beck

Maps: AURAS Design.

Acknowledgments

BIBLICAL ARCHAEOLOGY SOCIETY is grateful to Carol Andrews, Laurie Andrews, Coleta Aranas-Campanale, Robin Cather, Steven Feldman, Lauren Krause, Susan Laden, Cheryl McGowan, Michael Shoemaker, Suzanne Singer and Judith Wohlberg for their careful and devoted work in preparing this book for publication.

Index

(Bold face numerals designate illustrations)

This book began as an all-day Smithsonian symposium in Washington, D.C., organized by the Biblical Archaeology Society to deal with some of the most critical and hotly debated issues involved in the origins of ancient Israel. As matters developed, it is now much more than that, although it has retained much of the informality and easy understandability of an oral presentation.

The symposium text has been expanded, carefully edited, handsomely illustrated with maps, plans, illustrations (both black and white and full color), footnoted for students who wish to pursue any matter in greater depth, and indexed. In addition, the comments of three other leading scholars in the debate on the emergence of ancient Israel have been added, so that all sides have now had the opportunity to be fully heard. The core, however, remains the symposium presentations.

The symposium is introduced by Hershel Shanks, president of the Biblical Archaeology Society and editor of *Biblical Archaeology Review* and *Bible Review*. Shanks not only defines the issues, but provides the basic information needed to appreciate the scholarly debates. This is followed by presentations from three world-class scholars.

William G. Dever, professor of Near Eastern archaeology at the University of Arizona, directed the pathbreaking excavations at Tel Gezer in Israel and served as director of the William F. Albright Institute for Archaeological Research in Jerusalem. In his presentation here, Dever